Blogging for Income:

How to Make Money Online with Your Blog and Copywriting, Working Only 4 Hours During the Workweek. Change Your Habits and You Will Profit for the Rest of Your Life.

Table of Contents

Introduction

When it comes to blogging, a purpose for opening a blog can be different for different people. Plenty of people start a blog purely for personal purposes, but for a handful, the purpose of a blog is for business.

Your reason for choosing this book is ultimately to learn how to use your blog to make money, and that's what we are here to learn. Blogging for business or any kind of endeavor that could bring you money has an extremely pointed purpose- to place your website at a higher rank in Google SERPs, which also means it increases your visibility.

Your business relies on consumers to purchase your products and services. If you are a new business, you can use blogging to help you attract the right kind of customers.

Without blogging, your main e-commerce website will remain invisible, but with a blog, you can constantly add content to make it fresh, competitive, and searchable. When it comes to blogging for business, the sole purpose here is to connect you to your target audience.

The other reason is to boost your traffic and also to bring in relevant leads and audience to your site via your content. The more constant, consistent, and frequent your blog posts, the higher the chances that your website will be discovered and visited by a relevant audience. The more traction you get means that your blog is effective.

Blogging for Business

Doing a quick search on Google about blogging for business, you'd find queries related to making money through blogging. So you're not the only one looking to make money online and using a blog to do that.

The fact that plenty of them are looking for answers shows that not everyone has a definite clue on how much a person can make through blogging. Many of the results will tell you that you need to pay attention to key phrases since Google basically feeds on that. This is true, and a must-do, but there are many more things that you should be doing to make your blog profitable, and we will uncover all of these things in this book.

So back to the question- How much can you earn through blogging?

Let's look at famous blogs and how much they make to give you an idea:

- Bloggers Bjork and Lindsay from Pinch of Yum makes an average of $85000 a year in 2016
- Latasha Peterson of Arts & Budget makes $2,500 to $3,000 a month
- Make Sense of Cents's Michelle Schroeder-Gardner rakes in a monthly income of $125,000

- Harsh Agarwal or ShoutMeLoud.com pulls in $40,000 by blogging

So what's in it for you?

- Blogging is something you can do! If they can do it, so can you
- You need the right idea and the right strategies
- There is no stopping you!

Now that you know how much money bloggers make, this leads us to our next question:

How do Bloggers make money online?

You'd be glad to know that there are plenty of ways to make money using a blog: from banner advertising to affiliate marketing to selling your ideas, your products, or even offering your service. All of these are some of the amazing opportunities to make money.

So what is the best option for you? Well, the answer is- it depends on what you want to do and the kind of industry you want to be in.

What is Blogging for profit?

A blog is a web page or website that conveys any idea or thought and is regularly updated by the owner or admin. Typically, it is run by an individual with a particular approach or a small group having a specific purpose. Most of the time it is written in a light mode with conversational style or an informal way. If you are fond of writing a diary and want to share it online with a bigger number of people, you will be using a blog to communicate to the world and convey your thoughts on any subject. Thus a blog is a personal journal that is updated frequently and regularly and published online. As a short form of weblog, a blog is a spontaneous expression of your passions and thoughts.

Why blogging?

Another big question that comes up before us is why you need your own blog. Well, the answer is pretty simple. Every one of us wants to have a say and wishes to be heard by the others. Written books and other material needs investment and a lot of hassle. Getting things in print form is a tough job that involves time, energy, and of course, money and then your target market will be limited. But having a blog, you will be able to share your thoughts online and internet will spread your message to the entire world. You will find like-minded people with the same approach towards a particular issue or subject. With less effort and no money, your message gets hundreds of thousands of people. It is up to the blogger to post and share details of his/her daily affairs with the audience. There are many types of bloggers who blog about how they live, eat, and enjoy the pleasures of life and there is also a category of bloggers who use their blog on a specific subject they are enthusiastic about. Countless blogs on numberless topics on the internet are examples of the variety of blog topics.

Blogs on internet provide information about celebrities from different walks of life, beauty tips, politics, history, latest news on national and international level, investments, games and sports, wars and conflicts in the world, natural disasters, technical knowledge and home topics like cooking, gardening, interior designing, laundry machines, kitchen machines, and how the blogs teach the audience. Personal Blog are also popular among viewers and companies also use blogs to promote their products and keep themselves in touch with the customers.

Types of Blogging Platforms

Now that you know that you can make money from blogging, the next step is to choose the right blogging platform. This decision can be a little confusing to make, especially since there are plenty of choices right now in 2019. Blogging platforms have come a long way, and there are different kinds of blogs catered to the different needs and purposes for every blogger out there. In this chapter, we will look at the best (FREE!) blogging platforms that you can earn money from. We look at free platforms because all platforms are actually free to sign up and use at its basic level, or at least free for a trial period.

Once you start exploring and using its features, testing to see if this is something that works for you, you would get a good feel of how things would be suitable for your blogging purposes. Let's get into discussing the pros and cons of each of them. Firstly, here is the list of blogs we will be looking at:

- **WordPress.org**

- **WordPress.com**
- **Blogger**
- **Wix**
- **Tumblr**
- **Medium**
- **Joomla**
- **Weebly**

What is a blogging platform?

A blogging platform is essentially a place or a site where you can create and operate your blog site. A blogging software or service, on the other hand, is where you can publish your articles from- it is basically a content management system or CMS. In simpler terms, a software platform that allows you to create your blog post without any form of programming or coding knowledge is a blogging platform. As mentioned previously, there are plenty of blogging platforms out there, but you want something that fits not only your needs but also something that is widely used around the world. Here is a list of the world's most used blogging platform:

- **WordPress.org** - 48%
- **Blogger**- 25%
- **WordPress.com** - 13%
- **Drupal**- 3%
- **Joomla**- 2%
- **Wix**- 1%

- **Tumblr**- 1%
- **Medium**- 1%
- **Weebly**- 1%

The Best Free Blogging Platforms to Make Money

It is essential to choose a blogging platform that is popular as you can get plenty of tips, tricks, plug-ins, themes, and solutions from all around the internet. Also, popular blogging platforms ride high on search engine results.

- **WordPress.org**

WordPress.org is among the best blogging platforms out there, not only in 2019 but ever since blogs started becoming common in the internet space. At present, WordPress currently hosts more than 33% of websites on the internet. The reason for this is because WordPress.org is extremely easy to use. Apart from that, it also has a very helpful and active user community that has plenty of information, guidelines, and how-tos. WordPress.org, a self-hosted blogging platform, and open-source software.

The Pros:

- You are on one of the most widely used popular free blogging platforms in the world

- You get to build just about any kind of website you want

- There are thousands of free and premium themes you can choose from for your site design

- Access to about 54,000 free plugins to customize and enhance your site

- It is extremely SEO friendly

- It is also made to be mobile-responsive

- You get high performance with high security

- You also have access to tools that you can develop your theme to fit your needs

- *The editor uses a Gutenberg block*

The Cons

- *As WordPress.org is a self-hosted blogging platform, you need to be able to manage your blog on your own, and this includes backing it up and setting up additional security.*

The Cost

WordPress.org is free to use, but you also need a hosting provider that you can install and start building your blog. Plus, a domain name is also extremely essential. Hosting is pretty standard, and it usually starts about $3.95 a month, depending on the provider you choose. Bluehost or SiteGround is one of the best places to begin as a beginner. Both of these hosting providers are recommended with WordPress.org, and they also put in a free domain as well as an SSL certificate for free. You also have a choice of buying your own domain name as well as hosting providers, and if you do that, then your best option is to go with WordPress.org blogging platform.

- **WordPress.com**

WordPress.com and WordPress.org are two different platforms for blogging. This is something you need to know about the early on-set. So what's the difference? With WordPress.org, the CMS is where you get to develop or host your own blog with a hosting service provider. With WordPress.com, it is similar to other free blogging platforms where you get to create your own blog using their site. Plenty of beginners prefer to begin their blogging with WordPress.com because of its ease-of-use. Blogging is free with WordPress.com, but if you want their premium services and your very own custom domain name, then you also need to pay premium charges as well.

- The Pros:

- You do not need any kind of setup

- It is easy to use and manage your blog

- You can use the mobile and desktop apps to update your blog site from anywhere

- You own the content on your site which means you can switch it anytime, anywhere

- You also get free Jetpack essential features

- You also get 3GB storage space

The Cons

- You have limited options for customization

- You also cannot run your own ads

- WordPress.com does not allow you to sync Google AdSense

- You can earn money through WordAds

- Your account can be closed at any moment if you violate their terms and conditions

The Cost

The basic WordPress.com site is free, but you also end up with WordPress's very own advertising and banners. However, if you pay for their premium services, you can have your very own domain and get rid of their branding Ads. Their premium costs are $8 a month whereas their business cost is $25 a month.

- **Blogger**

Blogger is another popular option and a wise one to blog and to make money. It also has a huge collection of themes that you can use for free on your blog. It is also known as one of the best blogs for beginners. Just like the WordPress blogs, Blogger is free, but if you want their premium services, then you need to pay. For bloggers who use Blogger, your domain address would be yourname.blogspot.com, but if you pay for a custom domain name, then you get to customize your domain. This is the right platform for beginners, whether you want to use it as a personal blog or a commercial blog.

You can put in your advertisement so long as you are approved for Google AdSense even if you are on a free plan. This is one of the best free blogging platforms if you want to make money using Google AdSense.

The Pros

- Blogger is a free blogging platform

- It is also easy to use and easy to manage the site- you do not need coding knowledge

- You can use Google Adsense on this blog to earn money

The Cons

- You have limited options to grow your blog

- You do not have access to plugins or extensions to improve your blog's functionality

- While there are plenty of themes, it is not as varied as those on WordPress

- You run the risk of your account closing at any time if you violate their terms and conditions

- As you grow and start making money, you would want to expand your site, but you'd find that it is limited

The Cost

The Blogger account is free; however, it comes with limited options. You need to pay premium rates to have your own custom domain name. If using Google AdSense is your primary goal for your blog, then Blogger is the way to go.

- **Wix**

Wix is an upgraded platform in the world of blogging. Wix started out as an easy-to-use blogging and website option for you to create a free blog or website. You can use this like any other blog or website for free, but like all the other options, you need premium plans for a custom domain. Wix does not allow you to put your own ads in when you are on their free plan however it does offer you so much more capabilities of creating a full-fledged website with plugins and themes to make it professional as long as your imagination goes.

The Pros

- Wix is extremely easy to set up

- It is a great option if you are looking to create a website without any coding knowledge

- It's drag and drop elements enable you to build your site easily using the Wix Editor

- It is also mobile optimized and SEO friendly

- *Wix also has dynamic pages which means you can create the same single design for 100 pages*

The Cons

- Its free account has limited options

- Wix displays their ads on your website

- You only have one chance to choose a template for your site, and you cannot change it

- Wix does not offer other 3rd party apps

- Their e-commerce options are limited

- *It is not an excellent choice to make money, but it is a good option for a website*

The Cost

Their most basic plan is $5 a month, but it comes with the Wix brand ads and limited bandwidth. If you opt for the $14 a month, then you have their unlimited plan. Their VIP plan is $29 a month.

- ## <u>Tumblr</u>

The world's most popular microblogging site and social networking website. This site allows you to make the blogging experience different from the rest. Tumblr's community is very different from that of the other blogs with its community more into fandom, GIFs, bordering to eroticism, and loads of anime. Tumblr also allows you to use Google AdSense if you have a custom domain name, but it does not allow you to put in your own ad when you are the other on that blogging platform.

The Pros

- Tumblr is easy to use and free

- It also has integrated social networking into the mix

- It allows you to post multimedia from videos to GIFs in a short-term blog

The Cons

- Tumblr has very specific features to enable it to be a microblogging site so if you want to expand your blog; you need to go elsewhere unless you're happy with its microblogging capabilities

- The lack of plugins makes it hard to add in any additional features

- It is hard to transfer or export content from platform to another should you decide to move away from Tumblr and go on to something like WordPress

The Cost

Tumblr is free like the other platforms, but you have to pay for a custom domain name for your blog. You also need to pay for 3rd party apps to be able to use it on your blog.

- **<u>Medium</u>**

Medium is a very popular publishing blogging platform that caters specifically to long-form writing, with a niche audience of writers, journalists as well as story writers. Medium is free to use as well, but for readers, they would need to pay to read articles as there is a membership fee. You cannot put in your own ads unless, like Tumblr, you have your own custom domain. Medium is the long-form version of Tumblr, and it is a great platform to use if making money through writing articles is your purpose.

To become a Medium member, your fee begins at $5 a month, and it can go up to $50 a year, but the great thing is you get unlimited access to the internet's best writers, and you'd also get ideas that you cannot get anywhere else.

Medium charges a membership fee to support its writers the same way Patreon charges its members to support its artists and creative community. The membership fee is distributed among writers based on how engaging their content is with their audience.

The Pros

- Medium is extremely easy to set up and use. In fact, there is little to no setup required

- It has an easy to handle interface

- It is also free to use

The Cons

- The platform's features are limited

- You are not able to run your own ads if you use the platform for free

- If you lost your Medium account, you lose your followers

The Cost

As with all the platforms above, if you want custom features and upgrades, you need to pay for it. It is pretty standard.

- **<u>Joomla</u>**

This platform shares similar features to WordPress.org. It is also open-source, and it has its own Content Management System. It is a platform used commonly by non-profits, small businesses as well as large organizations depending on what their needs are. As of 2019, Joomla has over 2 million active websites. Like WordPress, Joomla also has extensions and plugins, and it is also a free blogging platform. You can also run your own ads on this platform which also means that this is another platform that makes it easy to make money through blogging.

The Pros

- You can work on an open-source software

- You have a search engine optimized out of the box

- They also have awesome design features and functionalities

- Pretty good security

- *An excellent option for making money*

The Cons

- As it is similar to WordPress.org, you'd be hard-pressed to put your finger on which one is better- making this choice could be hard

- You need to manage your own blog and website similarly the way you would with WP.org

- Joomla's community is much smaller than that of WordPress which means limited support and limited development

The Cost

You need a reliable hosting provider to host your blogging platform. Charges are about the same with WordPress.

- **<u>Weebly</u>**

Not to be confused with Weibo, this is another free blogging platform that is more of a blog site builder. It is one of the best platforms to use if you want to build an online store. You will also need a premium plan if you want to run an eCommerce business. For Weebly's shopping card feature to be added, you need to upgrade your plan to a Pro plan or a Business plan. They have the basic SSL security, and it also comes with 500MB of data storage. On the flip side, it has a subdomain, so if you want to have your own custom domain identity, then you would, of course, need to go premium.

The Pros

- It's an easy setup with simple drag and drop features and interface

- You have plenty of free blogging templates to choose from

- It is SEO optimized

- You do not need any coding knowledge

- The maintenance is minimum

- There are plenty of media and 3rd party integration options when you want to expand the blog's functionality

The Cons

- If you are on the free plan, the features are of course limited

- Since its media integration is robust, you might end up running into limited space the more media you upload

- You are unable to run your own ads to make money. Instead, their ads would be added to your site

- There is no phone support given to basic plans

- Migrating data and content from this blog to another is hard

The Cost

The pro plan comes in at $12 a month, but it is paid annually whereas the business plans are $25 a month, which gives you a free domain and a host of other new features.

Now that we have covered some of the internet's most popular blog sites, the next question to answer is:

How can I start a blog and make money?

Based on the comparisons given above, WordPress.org is by far the most superior and gives you value for your money. You can run ads for free, and you also have more control over your content. You can try and test out the other platforms but take note that in the event you do change your mind and want to migrate your content from other platforms to WordPress- you'd get into a whole load of inconvenience, a waste of time, effort and not to mention money. The more posts you have and the higher the traffic, the more likely you'd need a blog that gives you the added security, the expanding features as well as the necessary support.

So what do you do next to kickstart your money-making business through your blog?

It boils down to these next few steps:

1. Choose a blogging niche

2. Pick a platform
3. Pick a domain and hosting plan
4. Monetize your blog

So which blogging platform is best for making money? It all boils down to your purpose, needs, and of course, budget. If you are not sure, stick to a free plan first and explore the blog's features and then choose the one that best fits your needs.

Choosing to go premium should only happen once you have a pretty good idea of what you want in a blog even if you have the budget to go premium. This is because you would still need to invest time, energy as well as resources to put in the necessary content to see if the blog platform works for you or not. No matter what the decision may be, pick a platform that is easy to set up, reliable, secure, and has good support. All of this will benefit you in the long run and save you money as well as give you more headspace.

Other blogging platforms or websites that you can try are SquareSpace, Contentful, Yola, Jekyll, Ghost as well as LiveJournal.

What are the best blogging platforms for 2019, on the other hand, and which would be best for your business?

We put our money's work on WordPress, Blogger as well as Wix. WordPress.org is ultimately the way to go, and in the next few chapters, our focus will be on setting up a WordPress blog, exploring your niche as well as setting up your blogging business.

Fundamentals Of Blogging

The Challenge

For you to see the true results of what your blog can achieve, setting aside time and putting in a little effort can help you turn the vision of your creation into reality. Each chapter is a step in the right direction to turning your blog from a small profile to a valuable business opportunity or if you prefer to keep it at the hobby level, a profitable way for you to enjoy creating content you are truly passionate about. Over the next 30 days, it is time for you to commit yourself to this creative pursuit, every single day you will create an extra piece of content and learn a little more towards getting started with your first blog. There are going to be times where you might not feel like posting, you have nothing to add or you simply lose your passion. It is exactly for these reasons why we propose the 30-day challenge. To not only educate you through the process but also to keep that passion alive, that motivation burning and that inspiration flowing.

Right from the beginning, you will be filled with excitement and unwavering power to get started however this might start to dry up a week or two in and by the end, it might feel as though it is just another chore. This is where so many bloggers fall into the lower end of the income scale. They lose the fire they started with and eventually their blogging goes from a passion project to a business pursuit, to a job and finally just another note on the to-do list. It doesn't have to be this way. The reason why so many bloggers lose their vision early is that their lack of direction, they can't see where to take things next so they simply repeat what they have been doing. This, of course, gets boring and it is a good reason for the project to simply dry up.

This is where the challenge aims to change all that. To keep your vision alive, provide direction and of course to keep the blogging journey exciting every step of the way. The challenge will cover every aspect from where to create your blog, the theme to decide on, a niche to focus on, the content to be created, the sources of revenue and steps to drive traffic and scale your blog. We will also provide inspiration from some successful blogs, how they got started and what makes them so attractive to readers. These will show you, by just following through with your commitment, you can create an authority blog that may ultimately become your sole source of income.

Following the 30 day challenge, you will not only have a blueprint in place to continue to successfully build upon what you learned, but you will also have built a habit which is one of the best sources of discipline to keep you moving. If you have ever tried to pick up a new hobby or online income method before, only to have it fail to deliver results, it was never the method it was your approach. I say this because there are countless cases of people successfully apply exactly what you learned in their own projects and seen success. Blogging is no different if you really want to see your blog take off, commitment is key. Before you know it, you will start seeing results and while they will be small at first, they will build to something greater than you can ever imagine, simply by staying committed.

First Steps on the Path

Before you get started on your blogging journey, a firm understanding of where you are, where you are traveling to and everything in between will help manage your mindset and keep your motivation strong. Many aspiring bloggers might have expectations to create something, which will have the whole internet talking in just their first few days. Sure there are cases of this happening, but before you throw yourself deep into the hype, you want to first keep your head above water. Blogging can be an incredibly lucrative and rewarding experience, but setting the bar too high and letting your expectations run away from you can lead to disappointment and withering of motivation which can lead you to quit before you have even truly begun. This is something we certainly want to avoid happening since it can be avoided and instead, have you reveling in the small successes every step of the way.

By all means have grand goals in mind, such as building your blog to a certain number of subscribers on your email list or an income level you are satisfied with. Again these are grand goals, we can talk a little more about them later on in the book, but understand it will take time, effort and work to achieve these goals and for now it is all about having fun creating and expressing yourself through your new outlet.

This doesn't mean you can't start making money after a month of work, just understand, you are operating a blog as a business and businesses take time to nurture and growth before the fruit can be harvested. The last thing you would want to do is throw in the towel before your blog starts to see real success, this is where the 30-day challenge comes in to really push you past the most challenging end of the blogging journey, the first month. This is where a majority of the work is done and where the least reward is seen. But in no way let this discourage you after the first stages of the uphill climb, you start to see the view and it looks incredible!

Understanding Your Blog

What do you think of when you start talking about blogging? Do you picture writing posts about topics you are passionate about? Receiving free items to write reviews on? Or maybe you just

want your voice heard. These are all fantastic reasons to start a blog but let's first understand the current situation of blogs today.

In the early days of blogging, sometimes simple opinions could be voice and revenue was sourced from advertising. Of course, this was back in the late 90s and early 2000s when there weren't a huge amount of blogs available. These days, it can take a bit of time for traffic to flow to a blog and revenues from advertising are abysmal, especially in the beginning. We will focus on revenue generation a little further along, however, understand that most information you receive about blogging income is shrewd with inaccuracy mainly by bloggers who are focused on what used to work rather than being progressive and testing new waters.

Blogging is today's blogosphere (the combination of all online blogs) is a much more refined science. Blogging is generally geared towards complementing a business rather than being a revenue source on its own. This doesn't always mean you need to create a business along with your blog, however, your blog in itself needs to revolve around some kind of business in order to bring in significant revenue. There are many ways you can do this while still keeping your blog as your main profession, however never be afraid of branching out with your blog and creating a brand to complement it as this is where you can truly grow your influence and become highly successful.

Blogs can range from the simple online diary to a website dedicated to journalism or political commentary. While you can still build a successful blog around a diary based publication, this can take much more time to build up a readership and you need to have a distinctive voice to attract that kind of audience. It is difficult but can absolutely be done and in some cases, these can be the most enjoyable and satisfying since you only need to be yourself. For most of us though, choosing a niche in a topic we love is the way to start our blogging journey and for the purpose of this challenge, we will focus solely on this aspect.

Show Me the Money

Chances are your interest in blogging comes from one of the greatest human motivators in existence, the money. You have probably heard the stories of people quitting their jobs to blog full time, others making 6 or 7 figures just from their laptops or you may have even heard the many stories of people making barely a few dollars each month. There is no question that blogging can be incredibly profitable as well as a great chance to have the perfect work life balance. But what about the millions who can't seem to catch a break in the blogosphere?

There are many reasons why a blog might not make a cent or maybe just a little bit of ad revenue each month. One part of the reason is simply effort on behalf of the bloggers. I'm in no way saying these people are lazy or unmotivated, but not every blogger is writing every day to make 6 figures every month. In fact, many are just doing it as a hobby, for their own personal expression or simply don't have the time to invest in expanding their blogging revenue. There are also bloggers who are unsure of their next steps and try to hack away at their keyboard to have people click on the ads scattered around their webpage. So exactly how much can we make as a professional blogger?

A majority of bloggers, according to a survey performed by ProBlogger.com, can never reach the $100 mark, we are talking

81% of bloggers, 10% of these bloggers don't make a single $1 each month. If this seems a bit daunting, don't let it get to you. The reasoning behind this is many of these bloggers don't invest in their business or educate themselves on how to take their blogs to the next level, instead they stagnant at these stages and fail to move forward. On the higher end of the spectrum, 4% of bloggers make over $10,000 each month. So what is it that sets these bloggers apart from the rest? It has a lot to do with their expectations and what they aim to gain from their blogging business. Keep in mind, if these bloggers really wanted to expand their business and make a living from their hobby, they would find a way right? There is absolutely no way, they would take all the time to research the fundamentals and learn from the best, only to still be making under $100 each month. This is what will make the difference between a successful blog and one, which will always remain a hobby.

There is much to learn about the blogging business and this where education and researching what makes a profitable blog will be your key to being rewarding for your work. What a majority of these mediocre bloggers rely on, is the advertising revenue generated from their posts and the traffic coming into their blog. This is not the case, while you can make a revenue by advertising alone, chances are you will end up in that under $100 a month category. Instead, you will need to create content as a means of funneling traffic through to your business, where the golden goose egg will be offered for sale. Think of your blog as a platform for other income streams, a means of attracting an audience and not as a revenue source in itself. Advertisers will be attracted to blogs that can sustain themselves, not those that will have a few click-throughs each month. We will touch more on this a little later but it is important to understand, blogging can be incredibly profitable and lucrative if you understand the real driving force behind the business.

Where many bloggers can get discouraged is looking into these figures and feeling as though there is no profit to be made for their work, however this simply not true. Your blog is a business and the sooner you approach it with this mentality the sooner you can be rewarded for your work.

How to Build Backlinks

Here's a quick refresher of what we've covered so far for backlinks. First, you're unlikely to rank in the top 10 on Google unless you get as many backlinks. Second, popular blogs tend to get natural links by broadcasting their content to a large audience. Third, top-ranking pages generate new backlinks "on autopilot." Lastly, if you're starting out, you'll have to build links manually.

I'm not going to share every link building strategy because there are too many to discuss. Therefore, I will be providing you with the best link building strategies I have found based on my personal experience. The best link building strategies for blogs, therefore, are leaving comments, replicating your competitors' backlinks, guest blogging, and outreach. These strategies will be covered below in-depth in sections and in the following chapter.

Leaving comments is a great strategy to kickstart your link building efforts and help spread the word about your content. Blogs are not the only place where you can leave comments with links to your articles. Niche forums, online communities, question and answer sites (Quora), and even YouTube videos are all legitimate sources for you to comment on (if done right). Forum sites such as Reddit are great to use for comments if you provide value and then link to your article. However, on Reddit, it's key to not insert in a link to your article page every time you respond to a comment or you'll likely be banned, downvoted, or ignored. Quora is a bit different but is pretty much the same as Reddit. You should still be providing tons of values to those who ask questions but you can, but with Quora, you should insert links into every response of yours in a convenient manner such as by stating "click on this link to learn more" at least once or twice in your responses.

Find a few popular communities within your own niche and actively engage in them. Even if you struggle to find active relevant communities within your niche, you can still write comments in blog articles. When you leave comments on relevant blogs in your industry, it only works if you add the actual value to the conversation, much like Reddit, as blog owners do not want advertisers or people to leave their website to go to their competitors' website in most cases unless what you're providing is truly valuable to the conversation. As more common with Quora, the more regular readers you get, the more natural backlinks you will get. Although posting a lot on Quora and Reddit will likely not directly improve your Google ranking, it will help you reach a lot of people, convert them into fans, and then afterward, get some natural links from them which will eventually improve your Google ranking. Personally, I believe that leaving comments on relevant blogs and communities is the best way to kickstart your link building efforts. However, as obvious as it may be, ensure your comments are quality driven not quantity based.

How to Get Backlink Ideas from Your Competitors

Analyzing your competitor's backlink profiles can lead to a goldmine of link building opportunities that you would otherwise never be able to discover. However, some competitors have thousands of backlinks that you could never, statistically speaking, review and analyze them all. So how do you go about analyzing your competitor's backlinks without going crazy? Here are three great strategies I use that will allow you to make sense of such a large data set...

Strategy 1 - *Find their superfans*: On Ahrefs, go to the "best pages by backlinks" report after searching for your competitor's website and set "HTTP code" to "200 ok." This will list the pages on your competitor's website that have generated the most backlinks. Now, take up to ten of these pages (the links) and copy paste them into Ahrefs "*Link Intersect*" tool. Make sure to remove the "https://" from each URL and use the "prefix" setting which will give better results. I would select the five most backlinked articles on your competitor's website and then select the "Short link opportunities" button which should show you a list of websites that have linked to all five articles of our competitor. Because these "super fans" linked to not one, but five of your competitor's website links, it is likely that you can get a few backlinks from them as well. If you are a more established blog, it is likely that some of these websites already have links to your articles. Go back to the Link Intersect tool and under "but doesn't link to (optional)", enter in your website domain name. You can then see who is not aware of your content and attempt to get a backlink from them. If you go back to the Link Intersect tool once more, select "show me who is linking to any of the below targets", it will show you any website that links to any four, three, two, or even single, one of these articles.

There may be many trash, or just simply bad websites you find doing this process which you would not want a backlink from but there are numerous quality websites that would benefit your ranking if you were to get a backlink from them. You can usually identify trash websites through their domain name, content, website design, as well as website authority with a quick Google search. Keep note, that under the "intersect" tab it shows you how many articles are linked to your competitor, but not to you. If the "intersect" tab states "1", then they're not really "super fans" and you can probably ignore them. In short, you can scan through hundreds of websites in an hour and find good opportunities. Then, you can take five more articles from the blog of your competitor and put it into the link intersect tool once more to analyze their backlinks and continue this process with other competitors until you have a good database of "super fans" who are likely to backlink your content if you notify and/or contact them of your quality articles.

Strategy 2 - *Find the "power linkers"*: You can find websites that compete with a few blogs that you're competing with but have never linked to your own blog. Go back to the Ahrefs Link

Intersect tool and insert it into five well-known blogs in your industry but have never linked to your domain (insert your domain into the last box). This is a real goldmine of link building opportunities. All of these websites have mentioned content from all five of your competitors but have never linked to you. This has to change to improve your Google ranking. Simply contact them, provide them value, and ask them to link to your article. Many of which, if your quality is great, will link to you for free and with little argument. You can continue this process until your satisfied by playing around with the Link Intersect tool and by inserting in more of your competitor domains into the tool. You should be able to discover a ton of backlink opportunities with just a couple of hours of research.

Strategy 3 - *Analyze their latest backlinks*: Going back to the last two strategies, you should always look at the date when the linking websites were last updated. Chances are, many of the websites that linked to your competitors did so some time ago. In addition, it's possible that they are not active anymore on their websites. Therefore, the chances of them linking to you and responding to your requests drop significantly. This is why you should focus on the most recently acquired links of your competitors. Going back to Ahrefs, on the left side menu, there is an option called "new backlinks" which you should select after entering in your competitors name into Ahrefs search bar. I usually just scroll down after doing this and look for domain names that look good (short, simple, understandable). You can identify whether they've mentioned your website by searching in Google: ["site:enterwebsitehere.com" "your website name"]. You can also go to Ahrefs "referring domains" under the left side menu, put in the domain name that catches your eye into the "referring domains" search bar and verify that they have never linked to you. If they have not, you can contact them and notify them of your website and chances are likely that they may link to your content in the future for free.

With Ahrefs, you can also receive email alerts every time your competitors get new backlinks. Just go the *Alert tab* on the very top of Ahrefs, click on the "Backlinks" tab and click "New alert." If you're targeting a larger competitor, then you will get spammed by messages for every backlink your competitor receives. Therefore, I would suggest setting up alerts for a bunch of individual articles from their blog instead of that you care about the most (articles that are currently outranking you on Google search). This is an extremely useful tool and idea that I hope you implement.

How to Build Links via Guest Blogging

I'm about to teach you a few tactics, some of which are advanced. However, it's important to remember the fundamental of your blog, and that is that the quality of your content always comes first. In other words, the fundamental rule of content marketing. Remember, if you're content is top-notch, you will get astounding results with little effort. With this in mind, let us discuss the two most common challenges in guest blogging, running out of blogs to guest post for and understanding how to create more quality guest articles in less time.

How to never run out of blogs to guest post for: Most guides to guest blogging will tell you to use advanced Google search operators for finding blogs to guest blog for. They will tell you to do things such as run "special" searches in Google, scrape all search results, save them into a spreadsheet, run de-duplication, and then pull SEO metrics. All of this, however, is too troublesome. So, here is how I get a huge amount of guest blogging prospects in five minutes or less. On Ahrefs, go to the *"Content Explorer"* tool and put your topic there. In fact, you can put any keyword you determine blogs in your industry are likely to mention. Blogs in the SEO industry, for example, talk about link building, keyword research, SEO audit, anchor text, etc., which are all keywords you can insert into the Content Explorer tool on Ahrefs. Search for your keyword and begin filtering your results. Begin by selecting the "one article per domain" option which targets unique websites that mention the keyword you searched for. Next, filter the language to English (presumably). Finally, if you're not confident with competing with larger industries select the domain rating (DR) and have it set to between 30-50 so that you are only targeting mildly popular blogs. This will narrow down your results significantly, and because we know that their domain rating is not too strong, these websites are more likely to accept your guest article.

You can always adjust the domain rating filter appropriately to match where you are in blogging and who you want to target to attempt to guest blog for. You can also search for other keywords if you're not satisfied with the results you see. I would also suggest attempting to search for keywords that are not so closely related to what you do. You could actually go much broader than your niche keywords and still receive decent results. In the end, with this strategy, you should end up with a never-ending supply of blogs to guest post for.

However, how do you know these blogs allow guest posts? There's no real way to do this, just use your reasoning. Even if you don't see any other guest posts, there's no harm in contacting the blog owner, showing them your blog, and asking them if you could guest post for them. Even if you are turned down, you still put yourself on the radar of a prominent person in your industry. You can also improve your chances of gaining a guest article post by first getting the attention of the blogger through insightful smart comments on their articles and then offering to write a guest post for them (for free of course). This works almost all the time.

The second question you may be asking is "why should I publish articles on low DR blogs? Doesn't low DR mean that a link from them has little value?" Technically, from Google's prospective you're not getting a backlink from a domain, you're getting a backlink from a specific page. That is just how their page link works. In addition, larger DR blogs may have a bunch of weak pages while a small new website can have a few very strong ones. Besides, some of the small ones may eventually grow into much larger ones as well. Therefore, you shouldn't shy away from guest writing for a blog just because their DR is low. A better question to ask is "do I think this blog will still be around in three years from now?" If the answer is yes, go for it, and ask the blogger if you can write a guest post. If not, then don't waste your time writing quality guest articles that will disappear without a trace. Obviously, you should aim to publish guest articles on the very best blogs in your industry, which you may already be familiar with.

How to Build Links & Promote Content via Blogger Outreach

"Outreach" for Content Promotion

Outreach is not a digital marketing strategy. Influencer marketing, guest blogging, broken link building are all digital marketing strategies or tactics, whereas outreach is when you reach out to those who are connected to these digital marketing strategies. There's no such thing as an ultimate guide to outreach. It simply cannot exist because there are too many cases to consider. Therefore, I will focus on discussing how you can use outreach to spread the word about your content and landing high-quality backlinks along the way. First, let us tackle three things that people usually get wrong in outreach...

1. *Outreach IS content promotion*: Imagine this scenario. You emailed 100 people in your industry with a link to your new article. 80% opened your email, 30% clicked your link, 10% emailed you back, and 0% tweeted or created backlinks to your content. Most people, in this case, would probably assume this email marketing failed because it "didn't work." But think about it this way – by having an email open rate of 80%, your putting yourself in front of 80 people who are familiar with the industry you're in. The 30% shows that they may have an interest in your blog and

may have even read your new article. Finally, the 10% reply rate means that you just made a connection and networked with ten amazing people who are in your industry – which, as learned in previous chapters, can often lead to tons of potential benefits. Despite not getting any tweets or backlinks, it would be wrong to say that your outreach has failed as long as your emails have some traction to them. Again, this is why outreach should be considered as content promotion to you.

2. *There's a fine line between outreach and spam*: If you send thousands of emails in a month, in almost all cases that is spam. There's no way you can send personalized emails with every email you send, along with collecting and researching that many people to send emails to. Instead of sending thousands of emails in a month, it's much more beneficial and achievable to send thousands in a year with much higher quality writing. Put outreach and spam on two opposite spectrums. The difference between each one represents the amount of effort you put forth into each individual email that you send. This includes finding the person you want to get in touch with, researching them to see if they are a good fit, and obviously writing a personalized email to them. On the spam side, we would probably have an auto-generated list of people

with no manual review and probably a generic outreach template which you would copy and paste, changing up a few things afterward. This approach is pretty much the definition of spam and will not bring you the full benefits of outreach.

On the other spectrum, we have outreach. This is where you have a small list of people who you have thoroughly researched which enables you to write a unique and personal outreach email to each of them. But in all honesty, both ends of the spectrum (spam and outreach) are extremes that you should stay away from! You don't want to send thousands of people a generic email template, especially if you care about your reputation in that industry. At the same time, you don't want to spend weeks researching people and crafting the most perfect outreach emails possible, just to realize they're too busy right now for something you are sending them. The right approach, as you may have guessed, is somewhere in the middle – leaning more towards the outreach end of the spectrum. Each industry is very different, and I would suggest you play with how much effort you put into every outreach email before finding where to settle.

3. *Perfect outreach doesn't guarantee results*: Don't spend most of your time when you do outreach crafting perfect emails. It's quite a common scenario that the people you reach out to will be quite too busy to respond. Obviously, this is because life gets in the

way...what time of day does the person see your mail? Will they open it on their mobile phone or desktop computer? Are they in a good mood? Is there a schedule full right now? How many other emails have they received today? And the list goes on because there are a hundred emails your perfectly crafted email may not even get a proper response. You need to mentally prepare yourself for this and not get discouraged with your emails.

How to Find Thousands of High-Quality Outreach Prospects

Obviously, your primary goal of outreach efforts is to build backlinks to your content. As for promoting content, it's a natural byproduct of your outreach efforts rather than the primary goal. So, who should you reach out to? Who are the people who are likely to link to your content? Well, that would be people who have linked to existing articles on the same topic (that you've written about) and published articles where they may have mentioned that topic. These are the perfect outreach targets because they have a website to link from and they have an interest in your topic. Now, let me show you how you can go about finding these people...

Group 1 - *People who have linked to existing articles on the same topic*: If the people here have previously linked to articles on a topic you've written about, they might as well link to yours too.

That is, of course, if your article should be somehow better than the ones they are already linking to or offers a unique perspective. Otherwise, they just won't care. The best place to start is Google, by searching for the topic you want to rank for. You should then see who ranks at the topic and then look at who's linking to these top rankers on Google. Use Ahrefs *"Keyword Explorer"* tool to do this. Search for a keyword, scroll all the way down, and look at the "domains" column to see how many backlinks it has (while also noticing the ranking of the article on Google). Click on a number under the domains column for a website that is ranking well and one that has a significant number of backlinks and you will be redirected to the "referring domains" tool within Ahrefs explorer tool. This is where it should list all of the pages from where the backlinks came from. From here, turn on the "do follow" filter and order your list so that "do follow" is at the top (pointing upwards). Then, use a classic approach and look for domain names that make sense. By clicking the backlinks dropdown for any website listed here, you can see where exactly they are linked from. By going through these backlinks through domain names that make sense (to be linked from), you can easily scrape a huge list of websites that you can then outreach to. By searching for other relevant keywords to the topic your articles are based on in the Keyword Explorer tool, you can continue to grow your targeted outreach list.

Now, let me show you another cool method I use to find articles on the same topic as yours, that have a lot of backlinks to piggyback from. This time use Ahrefs "*Content Explorer*" tool and search for a keyword that is included in the title. Play with the referring domains option, and you can set it to domains that have a minimum of 20 referring domains to narrow down your results and to find websites that have a decent number of backlinks. You can then order this number of results by linking websites (referring domains). Glancing over your results, I hope you will see that you will find articles and websites that you may have not found by just using the Keyword Explorer tool in Ahrefs. This will give you many more unique outreach opportunities that you can then take advantage of. If you have an eye on a competitor website, you can also set up alerts through Ahrefs when they add a new backlink and get an email notification whenever they do. This is pretty simple to do, and I would suggest setting it to weekly email notifications.

Group 2 - *People who published articles mentioning your topic*: Chances are, there are a ton of people who have published articles mentioning your topic but have never linked to any other websites. Use Ahrefs "*Content Explorer*" tool and search for the keyword you want. Instead of searching for "in title", this time search for "in content". Afterward, select the checkbox "one article per domain" to search for unique websites. You can also filter by language to focus only on English articles. By changing the domain rating minimum to 70, for example, you can focus on popular websites only and can reduce this rating to focus on less popular websites. The lower the domain rating, the higher the chance to impress them with your content and persuade them to link to your content. Alternatively, you can filter by organic search traffic. I would go the extra step and try a bit harder when you do outreach for these high organic traffic websites. Finally, if you're a more established blog, you can use the "highlight unlinked domains" filter to differentiate between websites who have already linked to your website before and those who have never linked to you. Of course, reaching out to those who are more familiar with your content and have linked to you before, you are more likely to gain a backlink. However, remember that the more backlinks you get from a website, the less valuable it becomes to Google. In conclusion, this is how you will find people who have previously mentioned your topic in their articles.

Once again, you can easily keep an eye on the newly published articles that mention your topic with *Ahrefs alerts*. Go to the Mentions tab, click on the "new alert" button, put your keyword there – maybe even implement the "OR" operator to specify a bunch of them in quotation marks, select where you want to look for it (title, content), set blocked domains to your own domain or YouTube, for example, and set it to daily email notifications. Think about it, being a blogger yourself, you will be less excited when people reach out to you months later. However, when you publish a new article and people reach out to you within days or even hours, you will be very open to conversation! This is why it's important to use alerts in your marketing strategy and act on new outreach opportunities as soon as they land in your inbox.

Group 3 - *People who tweeted articles on that topic*: Search for your keyword once again in Ahrefs *"Content Explorer"* tool. You can easily see the number of times an article had been re-tweeted, Facebook shares, etc. after searching for a keyword through the Content Explorer tool. You can click on these numbers and it will redirect you to a Twitter search for the article URL showing you who tweeted it recently. Or, you can simply click the "who tweeted" button in the Content Explorer tool straight from Ahrefs own database which you can then easily export. You should be then reaching out to these people. However, don't focus on this strategy too much. If you get an outreach for someone on Twitter notifying you that you linked to an article on the same topic three weeks ago, most people would just ignore your outreach. This is because when someone tweets something, it's likely that they will forget about that article or what they even tweeted about in the past few days. In addition, stating "you tweeted a similar article" when doing outreach on Twitter, is a super weak outreach excuse for anyone to care about. Especially if the tweet was sent a long time ago. Instead of tracking people who tweet articles or have in the past, you should track those who have recently (one week or less) linked to an article similar to yours and perform outreach by just replying to their tweet. Say something along the lines of: ["Hey, that's a great post! You might want to check out this one too: "link". It talks about (...) which wasn't covered in the article you tweeted"]. This is more of a social media engagement strategy rather than an email outreach strategy, however. I would suggest you try both email and social media strategy methods and see what works for your industry.

Blog Content Creation

There are lots of ways to gather blog content. It is important that you have blog content that is up-to-date and new so that people keep coming back to your site. There are several ways to do that.

Write Your Content

The first way to build a blog is to write it yourself. This is the best option. You want to create blogs that are rich with keywords that are also interesting and unique. When you are starting out, this is the best way to gain credibility as a blogger. When you launch the website, you want to have five to ten blogs already on the website so there is content for people to read as soon as you launch the site.

The difficulty with writing a blog is that you want to tone to be authoritative and still create a personal connection to your audience. It needs to be full of useful information and entertaining to read at the same time.

The good news is that blogs do not have to be long. Blogs that are about 400 words are the most ideal. You want to make sure that you structure these blog posts right as well. They are different from article writing. Blog posts are engaging, thoughtful, and ask questions. The better quality your content is, the more traffic you will have to your blog.

You want to create a loyal following of your blog. These are the people who will bookmark your blog and come back on a regular basis to see what is new. These are the people that you are looking to engage the most with your writing.

Private Label Rights (PLR) Content

If you do not have the time or are not interested in writing your own content, you can use PLR content. This content is already written and comes as articles, ebooks, videos, etc., that you are able to use as if it were your own. Often you have to pay for it, but there is free material out there as well.

Since this is pre-written material that anyone is able to use, it is possible for it to be on other blogs as well so you want to spend a little time rewriting it. You want to rewrite anywhere from 25 to 30 percent of the article so that it sounds more unique than other material available.

Outsourced Content

There is an abundance of freelance writers you can hire to write the blogs for you. There are many communities on the internet where you can hire writers for decent prices. However, it is important to not base your freelance hiring decision only on price. You want good quality material so make sure that you are hiring a quality writer.

You can hire freelancers from websites like WarriorForum.com, Fiverr.com, and Guru.com. Fiverr.com is unique because you are able to hire good quality writers for five dollars. Guru.com provides some of the highest quality freelancers on the market. Make sure to take a look at past feedback for the contractor. That is the best way to know how competent the writer is and what quality you can expect.

Income From Blogs

There are several ways to make money and different ways to make your blog make money. A great way to get income from your blog is to add an opt-in form on your blog. This is going to provide you with a list of prospective clients.

This is a good way to get people to provide their email addresses, but you often have to provide something in return. By providing a free offer like a free ebook, ecourse, or some other informational guide of some type, you are going to entice people to provide their email address. You can put your offer on the blog an insert an opt-in box under it to get people interested in providing you with their information.

By building a list of people who visit your website, you are building a customer list that allows you to email these people directly about offers, affiliate information, and other information that your visitors may be interested in learning about.

To make this work, you need some tools to help make this happen. The first thing you need is an autoresponder. You can find these at GetResponse.com and Aweber.com. The second things you need is a squeeze page template that allows an opt-in form. This can be found at WhiteLabelReports.com. The last thing you need is an incentive. This can be reports, books, tutorials, videos, anything you can offer your visitors that will entice them to want to subscribe.

There is an opt-in box plug-in available for WordPress at CodeBanter.com that can help make it easy to enter an opt-in box on your blog.

This types of promotion make it easy to start developing a customer base from the first day your blog is up and running. You need to make sure that you put some thought into the "opt-in bribe." This is the bait that gets people to subscribe to your website. This is going to get people to want to become newsletter subscribers.

One way to get a hold of a great opt-in bribe is to purchase a good quality report from a website like CompleteStartups.com. Here you can buy a good report that is useful and interesting that pertains to your niche. Another way is to hire a freelancer from a website like Elance.com to write it for you.

It can save you time and money if you can write the report yourself. The most important thing to remember is that you need to offer something valuable to your customers that they want to read and are relevant to your blog.

As soon as the report is ready to be sent out, you can create an autoresponder account so that it automatically sends out an email when the person signs up. This is a welcome email. It will also thank the person for subscribing and provide the download for the report.

You need to make sure that you build a relationship with the people on your list. They need to know they can trust your content. This means knowing that you are providing sound advice, giving good tips and pertinent information to them. You can do this by spending some time with the people who are subscribing to your site through free material, responding to comments, providing resources and tips via email that can help them out. Providing them with free material is a great way to get them engaged with you.

This kind of relationship building will provide you with a loyal following that will be engaged in your website and interested in what you have to say. This also means that they will be interested in the products you have to offer them on your blog.

Affiliate Programs

You can also utilize affiliates through reviews. Writing a product review is a great choice for engaging affiliates. When you do a review, make sure that you provide a description of the product, the advantages and disadvantages, and how the product was able to help you. Then you want to include the affiliate link where people are able to buy the product. You want to make sure that you incorporate the disadvantages as well so that it makes the review more credible.

Clickbank is a great source for an affiliate network. They only sell digital mediums like video tutorials, ebooks, software, etc. This means they have lots of products that can be promoted and they payout 65 to 75 percent in commissions. This averages to be about $30 per sale. You can sort through the various offerings on Clickbank to see what they have available that meets your blog market. To get an idea of what products fit your niche with Clickbank, you can use a website called CBEngine.com to help.

Commission Junction is another possibility for affiliates. This has a large variety of product possibilities. They sell both physical and digital products and you can get paid per lead or per sale.

Amazon has one of the largest online retail stores available. Amazon makes it easy to review a site by using the HTML and templates for reviews that you already use. Before you can work with Amazon as an affiliate, you need to sign up for an Amazon Associates account with them.

Ebay works quite similarly to Amazon. They have many products that can be promoted on your blog and they offer a Pay Per Click program as well.

The question then becomes, how do you pick a product to promote on your blog? As an example, let's look at Clickbank. You would start by clicking on their marketplace link and searching for products from your keywords. This is going to provide you a list of products that you are able to promote. Make sure to look at the stats that are provided to know how the recent sales for that product are doing. You want to find a product that is moving well so that you get a higher conversion rate. Conversion rates are the number of people that buy the product after looking at it from your blog.

Just as with content, quality is important so make sure that you are promoting high-quality products on your site. You also want to make sure that the product price is in the range that your particular audience is willing to spend. You cannot just rely on high ticket items that have high commission rates.

Make sure that the products you are promoting fit in your niche market and not to the general market. This will help keep your blog targeted and focused.

Write Reviews for Affiliates

Writing reviews of products is another way to get affiliates to pay you. This involves writing keyword rich reviews that promote a product and directly link to that website.

Just as with any other blog content, you need to make sure search engines can find it and cater to those who read your blog.

You always want to write for your visitors first and search engines second. Visitors are the ones who are going to make you money. That does not mean that you cannot rely on search engines as well so you need to keep both in mind when you are writing content and reviews.

Incorporating keywords into the review is the best way to get the review optimized. Make sure that you are incorporating keywords into various areas of the review like the title tag, page description, meta description, anchor text, and alt text if you are using images.

There are goods ways to structure reviews and bad ways. You want a structure that is easy to read, looks nice and provides a good deal of information to the reader. Using images is great as well to provide a complete package to the reader.

Keep in mind that it is your job to inform the visitor to the site. You want to cover as much valuable information as possible for the reader. Keeping them casual will help to make the reader feel as if you are talking just to them, giving purchasing advice. People are coming to your site because they need answers and directions.

A review needs to be honest as well. You want to push the positives of a product to generate sales, but you need to appear to be looking out for the best interest of your readers as well. This is an important characteristic of reviews. Readers need a trustworthy, honest place to get information and reviews.

You always want to include some disadvantages to the product as well. This is going to make the review stronger and more credible. No one believes a product is perfect. This will make people view you as an honest source of information.

Reviews cannot be just product descriptions. You need to make sure that you are giving detailed information about the product. People can read the sales page on the product website; you need to provide more than that.

End the review with a strong conclusion that tells the person what to do. Do this in a non-aggressive way by making it a "when" statement. Say something like "when you purchase this supplement, you will weight and gain self-confidence." This tells the reader they have to have this product. You do not want to leave them with an "if" statement because that gives them a choice to not purchase the product. You do not want to question if they will buy it, you want to support the idea that they will buy it.

It can sound daunting at first but the more you write reviews, the easier it gets. Some of the affiliate networks out there, like Clickbank, offer scripts to help effectively write reviews. You can also use resources like reviewsscript.com or instant-sites-launcher.com.

Amazon Affiliate Program

aStores are featured products that are chosen by Amazon so you can easily customize your product offerings to various markets. You start by logging in to your Amazon Associates account and choose individual products or categories that you want to offer. All you do is insert the provided code into your blog and your aStore will appear on your blog.

You can also utilize banners and links for projects on Amazon. You can add them throughout your blog so people are able to click on the advertisements and be taken to the page to purchase the item. You can get up to 15% of sales this way.

Widgets are a great tool as well. These are small applications that can be added to your blog. They make parts of your blog as functional as the Amazon website.

When you are using Amazon Associates, make sure that you are readily checking your reports to know how your earnings are doing and they will provide you with information about how your affiliate program is going.

Google Adsense

This is a great option for people who want to get ads on their websites. You apply for the program and get approved by Google. Then you are able to get the code to place on your blog to list banner ads that people can click on. You get paid for every click. Generally, people get about 20 cents per click.

The more competitive the keyword is for the ad, the more you get paid when people click on it. You can get up to $30 per click depending on the competitiveness of that particular keyword.

Adsense is free to join and you are able to place the code for the ads anywhere you want on your blog, putting you in control of the advertising on your website. You can even customize the size, shape, color, background and scheme of the ads being placed on your website so they fit in with your theme.

This is a great tool because you make money just for the clicks on the ads. Customers do not have to purchase the items being advertised. This means that there is no commitment for you or your readers.

You are able to create several different campaigns with your Adsense account. This allows you to have several different advertisements over a network of blogs. This allows you to monitor which ads are doing well and which need some adjustment to work better.

Generally, larger square ads that match the colors of your website are going to do the best. You do not want advertisements detracting from your blog. You just want them easily accessible to the reader.

Begin with the 250 X 250 square advertisements. The 300 X 250 is a medium size if there is room on the blog for that kind of ad. If these do not work, you can incorporate tall, rectangular ads, called tower ads, down the sides of the blog. A 728 X 90 leaderboard ad is great for this type of display. It is good for the upper half of the blog right under the header or at the bottom of the page.

Make sure that you do not overload the page with the advertisement boxes. You do not want them to be the main focal point of the page. Your goal is to provide the best experience possible overall with your site so do not make it all about advertisements.

Make sure you are familiar with Google's Terms of Service as well. Google's Terms of Service state that you are not allowed to put more than three advertisements on one page. Familiarize yourself with all the restrictions before putting ads on your blog.

WordPress has a plug-in available to integrate Google Adsense into your blog. You will want to create different channels for each blog that you are going to feature Adsense ads on. This is going to show you which ads are working well and which are not. This provides you with information to change the ads as you need them to change in order to make them more efficient and provide you more income.

Marketing Your Blog

This is the moment you have been waiting for. After finally choosing your niche and setting up the website for your blog, you now await the coveted readers that bloggers have long sought after. Many novice bloggers' initial enthusiasm inevitably begins to wane after seeing a lack of traffic. While it would be nice to simply upload blog post after blog post and gradually build your audience, neglecting the basic marketing tactics will, unfortunately, leave you at quite the disadvantage. With so many blogs seemingly sprouting up out of nowhere these days with abundant amounts of free information, it can be difficult to differentiate yourself from bloggers just like you. Implementing the following tips, however, will help ensure that your blog receives more traffic than the alternative of not utilizing them at all. Ultimately, it is the building of an online presence that will be most conducive towards your success.

Participate in Relevant Forums

Regularly contributing in forums pertinent to your niche is a great method of building your online presence as a prominent blogger. Do not tarnish your reputation by promoting yourself through spam-like methods; instead, it would be most conducive for you to be legitimately helpful and genuinely participate. By establishing yourself as a respected member of the forum's community, members will be much more likely to take you at face value. That is, members of the community will not suspect that the only reason you are even a member of the forums is to promote your blog. Different forums will stipulate different rules regarding self-promotion, so do be sure to become aware of them lest your account ends up banned.

Participate in Other Blogs

This is similar to the previously mentioned point in which you participate in relevant forums. Consider contributing thoughtful comments on blogs related to yours. Do not simply post cookie-cutter comments such as "Great blog! I really enjoyed reading this post" and include a link to your blog. This is patently seen as a desperate, spam-like attempt to market your blog. Rather, strive to make a real effort in joining the communities' discussions and lending your opinion as well as insightful feedback that can potentially benefit the blogger and readers. If you can do this, then you have surely earned the justification to briefly include a backlink to one of your relevant blog posts. As a side note, it would be most effective to employ this strategy on the more popular blogs. After all, you would not want your valuable feedback to be for nothing on dead blogs.

Utilize Social Media

Never underestimate the power of social media, as it has the potential to significantly boost your exposure. Social networking has experienced tremendous expansion over the years and should be taken advantage of. Every successful blogger has prominence in the social media world, so it would be a good idea to emulate this. Of course, usage of social media accounts requires you to at least occasionally update your accounts to reap the maximum benefits. Every post you make on your blog should be updated on all your social media accounts to ensure that your readers know about it. By creating social networking accounts, this provides you with the opportunity to connect with potential readers that may have never known about your blog otherwise.

Create a Newsletter

Creating an email list should never be neglected, as most popular blogs incorporate this to remind readers that they exist. When someone signs up for your newsletter, that person is telling you that he or she wants to receive updates such as when you produce a new blog post. By giving your readers the option to sign up for your newsletter, you are making it easier for them to not only remember your blog but to tell their friends about it as well. Forget retaining your current audience: A newsletter can and will reach new demographics. This is because your more enthusiastic readers are apt to forward one of your emails to their friends. What about your less enthusiastic (casual) readers? They can likely be persuaded to join your email list by offering an incentive to sign up for your newsletter. Perhaps you are questioning the type of incentive you could possibly offer. Most bloggers opt to write a short eBook on something pertaining to their blogs and offer it for free to those who sign up for your newsletter.

Stay Consistent

Some bloggers will be ostensibly unwavering in their commitment to post on a fixed schedule and then randomly leave the blog without posting for weeks or even months on end. While consistency should be obvious, its importance cannot be stressed enough in order to keep the momentum of your blog going. Neglecting your blog whenever you feel like it will leave your readers wondering where you went. This is deleterious to the reputation of your blog including your own as a blogger. Readers would likely forget that your blog exists, and you can forget about the newsletter. Do not be surprised if readers begin unsubscribing to your email list, as they would have no longer have a reason to stick around. Stay consistent so your readers will see that you are serious and most importantly, reliable.

Incorporate Images

We are all visual creatures by nature, and the sparing use of images in your blog posts will liven up your blog while making your articles all the more pleasant to read. Of course, one should stray from using images found on Google to avoid committing copyright infringement. Your first thought maybe the incorporation of free stock images, but one should be careful here. It is more convenient and time-saving to use stock images, but you should ensure that your competitors are not using them as well. This is because some readers will inevitably notice the same images being used and may single you out as trite or lazy. If many other blogs are using those stock images, it would be a better idea to create an image of your own: a conglomerate of public domain/stock photos perhaps. Creating your own image is the preferred method, but a stock photo is not a bad alternative if it is not already being excessively used.

Guest Posting

Rather than writing content for your own blog, consider writing content for other people's blogs. This may appear to be time-consuming and a waste of effort at first thought, but this can actually be highly beneficial for your blog. If you have the opportunity to guest post for a blog with copious visitors, take it. Doing so will attract interest to your blog, especially when the blog is relevant to your niche. If the blog is well known enough, you may wind up receiving referral traffic from that blog for months to come at the very least. This is because you will have the chance to include a link back to your own website on your guest post, also known as a backlink. Backlinks will be explained in the upcoming chapter: Search Engine Optimization (SEO) Tactics.

Search Engine Optimization (SEO) Tactics

Now we get into the nitty-gritty of blogging: Search engine optimization. If you think you will be able to slide by as a blogger without learning about at least the basics of SEO tactics, you are going to have a bad time. In the most fundamental terms, search engine optimization is the visibility of your website in the organic search results of search engines, the visibility of which is affected by factors such as backlinks, domain age, traffic, etc. SEO also ties back to one of the benefits of having a custom domain, as Google does not favor subdomains or free blogs. If you have read this far and still are not convinced to opt for a custom domain, you may want to reconsider after reading this chapter and the importance of SEO. You do not have to be an SEO wizard by any means, but these are just a few SEO tactics a blogger should keep in mind for the sake of driving traffic to the blog.

Have a Custom Domain

You can tack this on as another benefit to having a custom domain: search engine optimization. There is some SEO research that suggests that having a custom domain will cause your blog to rank higher than if you were to opt for a subdomain. The increase in search engine reputation is admittedly arbitrary, however. While some blogs reap the benefits of a custom domain and notice more reader activity, other blogs do not experience this to such an extent. Regardless, looking at this from a practical standpoint, your blog will stand out in the search results more with a custom domain. Some believe that your own domain makes the blog more interesting and unique, and they may be more liable to visit your website when presented to them in the search results.

Original Content

Posting original, useful content is one of the most important things you can do for your SEO. Remember that Google wants to provide their users with the most pertinent and useful search results, which is exactly why you should strive to provide just that. If it is painfully obvious that you are simply copying the content of other blogs, the harsh reality is that your blog is not going to get very far. Let us say that consumers are searching for a solution to a ceiling leak. If your blog explains how to solve the problem in a cogent, original manner, it is safe to presume that your blog is going to be shared among readers. More sharing inevitably translates to a higher ranking in Google – this is why the type of content you produce is so important.

Blog Post Optimization

This should be a given, but you would be surprised at the lack of cognizance on the importance of the structure and style of your blog posts. To elucidate, this entails the incorporation of strategic paragraphs, headings for those paragraphs, bullet points (where applicable), and hyperlinking keywords or phrases to your other articles. Take a look at several prominent blogs, and you will quickly find that they use most if not all of the aforementioned elements. Noticing simple elements such as these in popular blogs will help you go a long way in your efforts to make your blog success-worthy. The SEO benefits may not be apparent at first, but boosting the appealing factors of your blog will increase the likelihood that others share your blog. Remember, the more your blog is shared, the higher the ranking of your blog in the search results.

Create Blog Post Titles Rich in Keywords

Each of the titles for your articles should have a more specific name for the post. This is because a vague title such as "A Few Recommendations of Mine" are too vague and do not give the readers any idea of what content the post contains in the search results. Potential readers are not searching for vague phrases such as these, anyway. Create titles for your articles that you think consumers are most apt to search for such as "How to Replace a Flat Tire." This will increase the visibility of your said blog post to the readers perusing the search results. To further accentuate the prominence of your blog titles, consider the following:

- *Use numbers where applicable in your titles:* This is recommended for the simple fact that readers are naturally drawn to titles that have a number in them such as "50 Ways to Make Money" as opposed to its duller counterpart "Ways to Make Money."

- *The first few words of your title are the most important:* The first few words of blog titles are more heavily weighted by search engines, so it would be wise to make them count. An example could be "Google Blogger: A Step by Step Guide." Remember: The keywords should be kept as close to the front of the title as possible.

- *Be descriptive and use adjectives:* Which group of words sounds more captivating to you? "Incredible, fascinating, and remarkable," or "great, cool, and fine?" Give your titles a little more pizzazz, and your readers will have a higher propensity of clicking the link to see what all the fuss is about.

Work On Obtaining Backlinks

This is especially important. For the uninitiated, backlinks are simply links on other websites that redirect to your website or blog. The more high-quality backlinks you have, the higher ranked your website will be in the results pages of search engines such as Google. As part of their criteria for determining the relevance of websites, search engines assess the number of quality backlinks websites have. Therefore, you should not simply be bent on obtaining as many backlinks as possible because search engines give more credit to websites that have the most quality backlinks. This means you should never buy backlinks, as they are not reliable and will likely be caught on by Google. The backlinks should also be coming from websites that are as relevant and popular as possible, as this will increase the quality of the said backlinks. The best way to go about this is to guest-post on blogs related to your niche and to continue writing high-quality articles.

Internal Links

Internal links are the links on your website that lead to other pages on your blog. Do not neglect hyperlinking certain words or phrases in your articles to other articles. This is not only for the sake of reader convenience, but for increasing the Google PageRank of the said pages. By building up the internal links on your website, this makes it easier for the search engines to crawl your pages – the implication being that your pages are more likely to turn up in the search results. By hyperlinking relevant keywords to other articles, those pages will be more relevant to the said keywords and phrases. For this reason, the blogger should ensure that the hyperlinked words are not simply "here" or other vague words, but more pertinent keywords that describe the content in the link such as "here are a few reasons to start blogging" or "SEO tips."

Say Goodbye to Writer's Block

The inevitable writer's block has stricken you, and you have run out of ideas for new content. What should you do? The longer you wait, the more impatient your readers become. They are waiting for you to release your next post; you must post something before you begin losing your readers! This runs through the mind of many bloggers, and we are all bound to encounter writer's block at one point or another. It is a frustrating time for many and can be discouraging to aspiring bloggers. Do not allow this to cause you to quit blogging, however, because even the most experienced writers will encounter a dry spell every once in a while. So what do seasoned bloggers do when they are not sure what to write about? They get creative and find ways to rekindle their creativity, of course. Here are a few tips and tricks for overcoming this hurdle when it arises so you can get back to pumping out fresh content.

Consider Your Audience

This should be one of the first things to assess when the creative well has dried up. You are thinking about your audience, are you not? If you have not already, consider the demographics of your readers. Place yourself in the shoes of your audience. What would they want you to write about? If you were an avid reader of your blog, what kind of information would you need or want? Surely you have had a desire for a post on a specific topic from another blog, so try replicating this thought process, only with your own blog instead. You may even consider mentally changing your audience so as to clarify your purpose.

Get Ideas from Your Readers

Who better to consult than the audience itself? In this case, you can let them do the heavy thinking for you. After all, the readers themselves will feel empowered upon noticing that you are taking some of their advice. Consider perusing the comments of your articles and seeing if any of them suggest ideas for new posts. If not, perhaps you could write a post asking your readers what they want you to write about. An alternative method to this is implement a plugin or button that reads "suggest a blog post," where readers can more directly offer input on what you should write about. Of course, you may not have a following sufficient enough to use this method. In that case, it would be preferable to use the other methods of generating content ideas in this chapter and returning to this option once you have amassed enough readers.

See What Others are Blogging About

Do what you must to keep your blog afloat, right? Keep up with your competition; see the content they are writing that seems to compel their readers to return. In fact, there is a good chance that this is what your competitors are doing as well. Everyone encounters the inevitable dry spell at some point. That is not to say that you should allow it to be obvious that you are getting your ideas from another source. Stealing others' content outright could get you in trouble with not only your competitors but Google as well. You can, however, take into consideration what other experts are blogging about. Then, you can incorporate your own twist and bring something fresh to your audience. For example, if your niche is in website design and you see a blogger with a post on how to use a certain program, you could make a post on how to go about that with an alternative program. The possibilities are endless.

Review a Product/Service in Your Niche

Reviewing a product or a service makes for a great topic for you to blog about. Have you purchased or tried something recently and would like to voice your opinion about it? Blog about it! As long as the said product or service is within the realms of your niche, anything is fair game. This is because when you review something that is relevant to your niche, your audience is bound to be interested to hear what you have to say. In fact, it would be wise to stray from reviewing anything that is not pertinent to the theme of your blog. Doing so will make you appear too self-serving, confuse readers, and ultimately cause you to lose some readers. If the product or service has left an indelibly positive impression on you, then this would be the perfect opportunity to incorporate affiliate links.

Write a How-To Series

After all, you are the go-to expert of your blog's niche, are you not? Since your audience is clearly interested in your niche, then there is bound to be something that they would like to learn about in your niche. This could go any number of ways; get creative with this one. Do you blog about your experiences with gardening and some tips and tricks you have learned along the way? Create a series of blog posts detailing how to grow certain vegetables, perhaps, and what pitfalls to avoid. Your readers will be refreshed to see a how-to series that is not blatantly deriving its ideas from other sources, and your blog will likely be recommended by them provided the content is quality. This is also a great method for churning out multiple blog posts rather than struggling to come up with just one post.

Blog about Current Events

If you are not already, keep up to date with information pertaining to your niche. There is no reason that you should not already be doing so; after all, you did choose the niche. Assume that you are blogging somewhere in the automobile niche. If, for example, an automobile manufacturer makes a controversial decision, this would be the perfect opportunity for you to write a blog post on your thoughts about it. In such a case, readers would undoubtedly be curious to hear what you have to say – especially when the more prominent and controversial any given event is. A general rule of thumb when it comes to blogging about current events is this: As long as it relates to your blog in some way, there is no reason you should not go ahead and write a post on it.

Take a Break Outside

Here is a piece of advice you may not have expected: Step away from the computer and take a break outside. Nature sparks creativity; this is common knowledge that seems to be overlooked by many for some reason. When all else fails in an attempt to find something to blog about, this is an indication that it is time for you to free yourself from the writing table and to clear your mind. The ideas may be locked in the back of your head, and the serenity of the outdoors could be just what you need to reel out these ideas. Embrace nature, even if only briefly, and you may find yourself pleased with what you are inspired to write about.

Driving Traffic

You can write for 30 days, 30 months or 30 years but if no one is coming to your blog, you are never going to make a cent and will likely get bored of typing to yourself before anything else. Driving traffic will give you that motivation to keep blogging, knowing that you have an audience eagerly waiting for what you have to say next. There are a number of ways to drive traffic other than the traditional approach of organic traffic, coming through search engines. Whether you want to use some of these strategies or all of them depends on the time you want to invest in your blog.

Importance of Keywords

Just as the title of your post ensures it will be clicked on, the keywords within your post and the title will help it show up in the search engines. This is known as Search Engine Optimization (SEO) with keywords being a major part. When you are searching through the web to solve a problem or learn something new, you will go for the keyword that best matches what you are looking for. Your blog should be no different. Keywords will also help you come up with blog posts that your audience will find. To get started with keyword optimization, think of a key phrase which best matches that your articles is trying to get across. Use this phrase in the title as well as throughout the post a number of times. When adding an image, include the keywords in the image as well. Finally, when creating the link to your post, add those keywords once again.

Social Media Marketing

Social media marketing has become an incredible powerful tool over the last decade. So much so that it has become an industry in itself. Social media marketing allows you to connect your niche through targeted marketing, following their interests and that of their friends. This means you can create campaigns and know exactly who you are targeting and where to find them. To make the most of social media marketing, it is best to create accounts relating to your blog across all social media platforms such as YouTube, Instagram, Facebook, LinkedIn, Google+ and Pinterest. This will allow you to share each blog post you create, every single day and increase the chances someone will see it and be attracted to the title. While the traffic will be small to begin with, over time you can have upwards of thousands of hits on just a single post.

Once you do have established social media accounts, you are able to leverage these not just to gain more traffic but also as revenue sources in themselves. Don't be afraid to get creative either, creating related YouTube videos.

Influencer Marketing

Obviously when we first start writing our blog we are not going to have a huge number of followers, this is where it helps to take advantage of someone who does. Influencer marketing has only revealed itself as a form of marketing very recently however it is one of the most impactful forms of marketing currently available to us. Influencer marketing is when you proposition a person who has a large following on social media, let's say for example, Instagram. When someone has a large following, it gives you the chance to expose your product or service to this number of people, without needing to build followers yourself. If we can think of a television program airing weekly with over a million viewers for each episode, advertising will quickly want to make use of this and will pay for their product to be featured on the show. Influencer marketing works very much the same way, with the person behind the social media accounting, giving a shout out to your product or service.

Here is a way you can get started with influencer marketing in the early days of your blog and start building your list. With your opt-in product created, find an Instagram account related to your niche. For example, if your blog is all about traveling while making money online, you can contact a traveling Instagram (you will need to find their email in the bio), and send them a request for a sponsored post. The costs of these can vary depending on how many followers they have. You will want your sponsored post to be advertising your free opt-in product. So if you have written an eBook advertise it as a free eBook for learning how to make money while traveling. Link the post over to your opt-in page (on your website) and in order to receive their eBook, they will provide yours with their email. This allows you to build your list to hundreds in just a matter of days. Of course, it does require the initial financial investment so whether you want to give your traffic a boost in this way it is entirely up to you. But make no mistake; this can go you on the fast track to progress in the early stages.

Guest Posting

Guest posting is one of the most effective ways of linking your blog with others as well as making some connections in the blogging community. A guest post is one that is written on behalf of your blog by another author. There are numerous opportunities for guest posting online and plenty to choose from especially if you wrote up a list of blogs you liked and felt they were similar to your own niche. While some guest post opportunities will pay you for your content, if you are just looking for a way to drive traffic to your blog, free opportunities would be easier to get into and more successful. Selecting a blog in your niche not only will allow you to keep their readers interested, but it will also help you attract new audience members since they are very much interested in the topic.

Having another author guest post on your own blog is also a great way to make new connections and link other blogs with yours. This improves your ranking in the search engines as well since your site has a greater number of links to other areas of the web.

Newsletter

Let's not forget all the hard work we did in setting up our mailing account, only to not use it for its primary purpose. Sending out your weekly newsletter is a great way of reconnecting with subscribers who may have only come with the purpose of getting your opt-in freebie. Your weekly newsletter needs to have a particular voice and speak to your subscribers directly. Start off by telling a short story about what may have happened in the week or something, which you feel, your subscribers would find entertaining. Remembering to keep it about your niche and avoid going off-topic because while you might be find the story of your dog's trip to the groomers, your subscribers may not. Keep it relevant and interesting.

Once you have written a little message to your subscribers, compile a set of links towards your posts throughout the week. This allows your subscribers to see what they may have missed throughout the week and will give them a chance to read up on something that catches their eye. MailChimp has a template for setting this out which allows you to add a picture relating to the post, the title as well as a short description of what the post is about.

Monetizing Your Blog

Your Own Product

The first way you should be monetizing your blog is with your own product, if you have one. If not, then no problem, as there are other ways to monetize your blog without having your own product that we're going to get into in this chapter.

If you don't have a product though, you should think about creating one. Your product could be anything from an ebook to a video course to some cool item that you make yourself in your garage. It's really your call what product you want to sell.

For most new blogs, creating a niche related ebook that your readers would be interested in purchasing would be the way to go at first, until you come up with another product idea.

If your product is an ebook, the easiest way to sell this from your blog would be to upload it to Amazon's KDP platform, which can be found at:

kdp.amazon.com

And then put a link to your ebook on your blog. The benefit of using a service like Amazon for your ebook is that you can also make sales from Amazon shoppers who might stumble upon your ebook when searching the Amazon store. Based on that, it's a good idea to make sure that you put a link to your blog in your ebook, so that anyone who hasn't heard of your blog who buys the ebook could easily click your link to find your blog and potentially become a follower.

Affiliate Products

The reality is, that you really don't need your own product. Many bloggers who earn an utter fortune blogging do it entirely by promoting affiliate products.

In case you don't know what an affiliate product is, allow me to brief you on the matter. An affiliate product is the product of another company that you put on your website, and when someone clicks on the link of that product and buys it, you get paid a percentage of the profits.

In order to promote affiliate products, you need to first of all join affiliate programs of companies that have affiliate products related to your niche. If your niche was meditation, for example, you would simply type in your Google search bar "meditation affiliate," and all affiliate programs related to meditation will pop up.

There are so many affiliate programs out there for almost every niche that you're bound to find something no matter what your niche is. Even Amazon has an affiliate program which can be found at:

affiliate-program.amazon.com

Just enrolling in Amazon's affiliate program alone will allow you to promote any product they have in their store.

Once you find an affiliate program that matches your needs, you simply want to register for it. For most affiliate programs this means filling out a form with your information, such as name and address, and also your bank information so they can pay you.

Once you register with an affiliate program, you'll then be given access to an affiliate dashboard where you can get affiliate links and banners. These affiliate links and banners are what you would put on your blog. If someone were to click on them and make a purchase, you would make money.

Now, you don't want to go wild and promote every affiliate product out there. You want to choose a handful of products that you are confident about that you can keep promoting, maybe around 3 to 5 affiliate products. And you want to put the affiliate banners to these products in your blog's sidebar and in your blog's footer.

You can put them in your blog's sidebar and footer by going to your WordPress dashboard and going to that big column on the left side, and hovering over Appearance which will cause a menu to pop up, and then you click on Widgets in that menu. This will take you to the Widgets page.

In the Widgets page, you will basically look for a block-like thing that says Sidebar, and multiple block-like things that say Footer Area. You should find these on the right side of the Widgets page.

On the left side of the page, you should see an Available Widgets section. What you want to do now is find a Text widget and then click on it and drag it to either the Sidebar block-like thing on the right, or on one of the Footer Area block-like things, and then release. It should stick there if you did it correctly.

Next you want to open the Text widget, and fill in a title for it and below the title you'll see 2 tabs, one called Visual and one called Text. You want to click on the Text tab, and this is where you'll paste in your banner code for your affiliate banner. Then you click the blue Save button below where you just pasted the code.

If you did it right, then when you look at your blog now, you'll see your affiliate banner there. This means you're set up to get paid.

I would recommend putting the same affiliate banners in both your sidebar and footer. Though it's up to you how you would like to do it. As long as they are there and are visible, then your blog is monetized from an affiliate banner perspective.

One last thing I should mention, the FTC has some regulations about disclosing affiliate links, and you need to follow them. You can find a link to information about disclosing affiliate links on the FTC's website at:

BloggerBlogger.com/

Now, I've never heard of a blogger ever being busted by the FTC for failing to disclose, but you don't want to be the first that it happens to, so I'd recommend you take some time and read about the FTC's guidelines about it to make sure you understand them.

Email Marketing

You only want to get into this once mastering your host, WordPress, and Google Webmasters, and once you notice a real following starting to grow on your blog, which should be apparent by people leaving comments on your blog posts or you getting some affiliate commissions from people clicking on your affiliate links and buying something. And if you've mastered those 3 things (your host, WordPress, and Google Webmasters), then you are ready for email marketing.

The concept of email marketing is rather simple, you put a form on your blog that promises some free piece of content to those who join your newsletter, and people write their email address in that form, and are then emailed that piece of content, and are now on your email list.

Once they're on your email list, you want to email them value, but at the same time, you want to email them affiliate offers. Remember all those affiliate programs that you applied for, well the ones that you didn't pick to be permanent fixtures on your blog, you should be recommending to your email list.

Once you get this system going, you are no longer simply running a blog, but you are now running a blog and newsletter. Of course, your subscribers expect you to email them things with value, and of course, you should also be emailing your list affiliate offers.

Everyone has a different approach to how to email their list, as in what percentage of their emails will be purely valued, and what percentage of their emails will be affiliate offers. And to find out how this is done, I would recommend that you find some blogs and stick your email in their form, and join a bunch of email lists and see what they send you. You can start by joining my list, which you can find at:

BloggerBlogger.com

But you don't have to join my list, it's entirely up to you. You can join any list that you want.

Anyway, as far as the lists you join, you want to study their email frequency, as in how often they are sending you emails, and you want to examine what kinds of affiliate offers they send you.

Now, that free piece of content that you first have to send to your subscribers, you're probably wondering where you get that from. Well, plain and simply, you make it!

In most cases that free piece of content, which Internet Marketers call a lead magnet, is a PDF document, but it could be a video course or a free piece of software that you built, or any number of other things. It's totally up to you what it is!

But if you don't know how to build video courses, and you don't know how to build pieces of software, then probably a PDF will be the ideal lead magnet for you. And there is nothing wrong with that, as many bloggers who are quite big use PDFs as lead magnets.

The way you make your lead magnet is you first of all have to think about what your audience will find value in. And once you have an idea, you write up the content, and then export it to a PDF document, there is your lead magnet. Really simple, huh?

The next thing you need to do is set up the technical stuff, the form on your blog and the software that will manage your email list. No, you can't use Gmail, or Hotmail, or Yahoo Mail, or any kind of regular email service to manage an email list. Because you need something powerful enough that it will let you hit one button and email thousands or hundreds of thousands, or even millions of your followers at once.

The good news is, that there are many companies that can handle the whole thing for you, meaning they can help you to quickly and easily get that form set up on your blog, and set up that first email with your lead magnet and help you manage your email list. These companies are called autoresponder services.

To find out the one I recommend, just go to:

BloggerBlogger.com

And look in the Essential Resources section for Tools, and click on Best Autoresponder, and you'll find my recommendation there.

One thing though, an autoresponder service is not free but is well worth the price. You have to think of an autoresponder as being like your mobile phone, you're going to pay a monthly bill for it, but you have an important communications tool that you can use to email your list whenever you need.

And the reality of the situation is, that you'll make more money emailing affiliate offers to your list than you will with affiliate banners on your blog or affiliate links on your blog posts. Sure you'll make some money from people who click those affiliate banners and links on your blog, but you'll make far more from your list.

Because email is a more personal experience than a blog, and so your followers are more likely to buy off of your recommendations via email. Don't ask me why, but that's just the way it is. I mean, look at any blog that's doing well, all of them have some kind of lead magnet that they're offering you to get your email on their list. Why is that? It's because they're actually making the most money off of their list. Most bloggers will not come out and say that, but that's the truth of the matter.

And the next and final piece you want to add to your continuous learning regimen is your autoresponder service. And once you have that final piece of the puzzle in place. Then you're going to do really well with your blog and with your newsletter.

This information I'm sharing with you is basically gold, so I hope you see the value in this!

Blogger Lifestyle

Once your blog gets off the ground and you're making money from it, it's time for a lifestyle change.

It's a personal decision as to whether or not you want to quit your job, and I wouldn't recommend quitting your job unless your blog was earning you far more than your job is earning you.

If however, your blog was earning you the same amount as your job, I'd recommend sticking with your job for now. And the reason I recommend to stick with your job is that your income from your blog is unstable; you might be earning the same as your job this month, but who knows where that's going to be next month. If you have a bad month, where will you be? You have to consider those things before just assuming that the income from your blog is just going to come in every month. However, like I said it has to be your own decision, and you are expected to do the math on it.

Though, whether or not you quit your job, you can still live the blogger lifestyle!

So what exactly is the blogger lifestyle, you might be wondering?

Well, it's basically living life on your terms, you go where you want to go, you do what you want to do, and you always carry your laptop with you and write blog posts! Now, I get that if you are still working at your job that it's kind of hard to really live life on your own terms. However, if you have days off, then you live life on your terms during your days off. If you don't have days off, then you live life on your terms after work. Whenever you have free time, you live on your terms!

This doesn't mean that you should stop writing blog posts, because sticking to your posting schedule is a part of the terms of your life that you've previously set. So technically, you are living life on your terms by writing blog posts!

So what do you do with all that money that you earn from your blog? Well, you do whatever you want with it. I recommend playing it smart and using it to create a bright future for yourself. If you have unpaid bills, you pay your bills with it. If you like to have a coffee while writing blog posts, then you buy coffee with it. You do anything you want to do with it and make sure you save a little bit of it for those times in the future where you might have bad months. The bottom line though is that you do whatever you want to do! I mean, it's your money, you earned it, right? So no one should tell you how to spend your money, only you can decide that. Just make sure you don't squander it on frivolous things.

I've known many a blogger who did quit their job because they had a good month, and they thought that every month was going to be like that. And they bought a new computer, and new clothes, and new sunglasses, and the following month was a bad month and they wound up not being able to pay their rent and ended up homeless. They had to live out of cafes and sleep on park benches until they could have some more good months where they were then able to get back on their feet. So don't be blindsided by the money thinking that every month will be the same. You should have some money saved up and your earnings should be well above what you make at your job before you even consider quitting. And most of all, don't squander your money, but don't be afraid to spend a little and enjoy life! After all, you earned a little enjoyment for yourself spending all those hours writing blog posts! Though just promise me that when you are enjoying life, that you're enjoying life on your terms! That's important!

However, yes, you're goal should be to quit your job at one point and blog full-time. After all, that is the dream!

Mistakes to Avoid

Not being careful of the scammers: There are a ton of people out there who are looking for ways to make money. They want to be able to quit their normal day job and just work from home on their own schedule. Because of all this desire, there are a lot of scammers out there who are more than willing to take your money, after giving some big promises, and then running away. There are a lot of great affiliate marketing companies out there to work with, but then there are a lot of scammers out there as well. If it sounds too good to be true, then it probably should.

If you are going through and the company is making big claims that you will be able to make thousands of dollars in a few weeks, then this is a sign that you should run away. If they say that you will only need to work for half an hour a day, or an hour a week, or some other silly claim like that, then it is time to look the other way as well. These companies are simply looking to part you with your money, and as soon as they have it, they will run away, and you will never be able to get ahold of them again.

In addition, reputable affiliate marketing companies are not going to ask you for any money to start. They may ask for a bank or PayPal account, but this is so they can pay you once you get some referrals on your link. If a company is asking for this information because they want to charge you, that is a big sign that they are fake, and you should look somewhere else.

Having only one source for affiliates: It is usually a good idea to have a few different locations online where you are promoting the products that you want to sell. If you just focus on a website or just on social media, then you are going to find that you are missing out on a lot of the customers you could be reaching. Many successful affiliate marketers are going to focus on at least two different options, and in the beginning, this may be all that you are able to handle because that is a ton of work.

Not maintaining a consistent brand: The fight isn't over just because you've gained a large number of followers. They can decide to stop reading your content at any time. That's why it's important to both peak interest and to keep that interest. To do this, you should stay true to the reasons these followers were inclined to follow your brand in the first place. Did they follow you because of the interesting infographics you posted? Then keep posting infographics. Keep feeding them the content they like, and they're much more likely to stick around.

You also want to post regularly. Whatever presence you have on social media should be dependable. This not only keeps their attention but again and again exposes them to your brand. The more familiar someone is with your brand, the more likely they are to become customers when they decide they need to have what you are selling. Post things that are closely related to your company's product or service. Share interesting things about your business and present them in interesting ways. Give them exclusive information, make your company seem transparent and honest.

Look for people talking about your brand. Do they have something positive to say about your company? Then Engage with the post and leave a comment expressing that you're happy you had a good experience. Do they have something negative to say? Then leave a comment inviting them to let you sort out whatever problem they have. Be honest about your mistakes and take great effort to correct them.

Denying a customer's problem is probably one of the worst things you can do for your brand. It makes your brand seem vain and close-minded. When someone communicates with a big company over social media and they get a response back, it often has the effect of making the customer appreciate the effort you expend for them. It makes them more likely to remember you and also more likely to engage again, which keeps their interest and ensures your content reaches them.

Not utilizing SEO correctly: SEO can be done on your own, or you can find sites that will do the SEO for free for you. One of the biggest benefits to this, of course, is that you will not have to worry about paying a dime for something that will help to increase traffic to your website. The downside is that you may not get the highest quality possible when it comes to your site. You may also not be able to get the most out of it or the same type of support that you would with typical SEO.

While paying for SEO may be an extra cost that you will have to consider when setting up your affiliate site, it is something that will be able to pay off for you in the long run. Even though it can cost a lot of money, you will have a higher quality SEO turnaround and your site will show up much better on the search engines. No SEO professional will be able to guarantee that your site will show up first, but someone who is good at it can make your site higher up on the ranking.

You will need to make the decision of whether or not you want to be prominent on the website. Do you want your affiliate site to be your face? If yes, you should consider the tone and the style of the site before you even begin putting it together so that you will be able to have yourself at the forefront of the site. It is a good idea to make sure that you are getting what you want out of the site and that it is truly working for you. You may also want to stay completely behind the scenes on your website which is also a great option for people who just want to use their site for affiliate marketing purposes. If this is the case, make your site more objective than it is personal.

Not using outreach and PR: This form of promotion is called "earned media" and it relies on you building quality relationships with people in the industry. You want to reach out to the media and bloggers and pitch the idea that they write about you. Whether you are writing to the media or to a blogger, you are going to first want to find out what the writer or reporter is interested in. Then, you can carefully generate pitches that are unique to the person you are writing to. You want to make sure that the pitch features something that they would find particularly interesting, without including everything you've ever created or accomplished in your life.

The majority of the time, the person you are pitching to will want something special in return for the exposure. The majority of the time the special something they would want might be early access to some form of important information, or another exclusive offer. Bloggers specifically may also be interested in receiving free goods or a special deal for their readers. Before you approach them, you want to make sure that you have reviewed any special submission guidelines they may have to ensure that your submission meets their guidelines and you are taken seriously.

It may feel uncomfortable directly reaching out to the media or to bloggers, but this is a great way to get your name out there in a major way. Some people may not be interested in writing about you or your business, but others likely will be, and this will give you a great advantage for marketing your business.

Not using the top SEO practices: Search engines are one of the best sources of gaining valuable, organic traffic of interested buyers. These people are actively seeking information related to your products and services, and as such are already halfway through the buying cycle. Your SEO practices should be top-notch to be found by those interested and relevant readers. Get into the habit of using H1, h2, and H3 (HTML tags). Ideally, the title tag should include a couple of relevant keywords.

Do not forget to include a meta title (which is nothing but the title appearing on your page in search results and not the actual page) of under 60 characters. The meta description (again the description of the page appearing in search engine results and not the actual page) should be below 160 characters. It should succinctly yet compellingly convey what the page is about, so readers have a good idea what to expect.

This practice also makes it simpler for search engines to locate matching content among millions of other pages and improve user experience by displaying the most relevant results. Include keywords naturally and wherever relevant to your posts. Do not create spammy, keyword stuffed articles in the hope of boosting your SEO. Few things affect your search engine optimization efforts as forced, excessive and irrelevant keywords. Affiliate farm blogs are heavily looked down upon by Google, and your site runs the risk of being permanently banned by Google.

Use long-tail keywords, especially if you have a very narrow and focused sub-niche that interesting a select group of audience. This practice will you access to audience/users who are already interested in buying or looking for exactly what you are offering. For example, if you are an affiliate to range for kitchen appliances, instead of simply including keywords such as "Belgian Waffle Maker XYZ", you can say "the best or cheapest price for Belgian

Waffle Maker XYZ" or "comparison of Belgian Waffle Maker XYZ with other Waffle Maker models" or "buy Belgian Waffle Maker at the best price."

Common Marketing Mentality Mistakes

- "Marketing is puzzling and totally unpredictable" - There are many, MANY marketers that come into the game with the idea that online marketing is a puzzling type of mystical game that they just cannot quite grasp. They like to think that some people have more of a "magic touch" than they do. But the truth is, marketing if done correctly, is highly predictable and easy to control

- "Marketing just isn't the right fit for my business" – The individuals who think this way have probably had a few goes around the block, having little marketing success. Due to this, they have become accustomed to the idea that marketing must not be a thing their business would benefit from, which is far from the truth. They have to realize that to grow their revenue, they must be able to successfully leverage marketing to their advantage.

- "I just suck at marketing" – And then there are some business people that shoot themselves in the foot with negativity before they even get started. Even the ones that have marketing down to science had to at some point learn, grow and improve. If we find the right guidance and learn how to acquire knowledge gracefully from our past mistakes, this can make anyone a very valuable marketer. You just have to stick with it! Patience is key!

- Success is never permanent, and failure is never fatal. This is a good quote to live by as a marketer, entrepreneur, etc. We eat, breathe and live from the mistakes we make, making learning curves constantly to stand behind in regard to our business no matter what that business might be.

Tips and Tricks

Think like your users

In the end, when you're doing affiliate marketing, you're trying to do one really simple thing: sell a product. The blogs are just a means by which to do that. However, there's a right and a wrong way to do things when you're trying to sell a product, and these are as true on the internet as anywhere else. In this chapter, I'm going to be giving you some valuable tidbits that I've collected which will help you to best market and sell your products.

Moreover, it makes them even less likely to return to your site, because they subconsciously feel like they're just going to have sales offers lobbed in their face. They're not wanting that. They're searching for something to buy related to your niche – they're looking to know more about it, first and foremost.

Keep that in mind: you aren't trying to sell them anything explicitly. You're offering them the opportunity to buy something, and if they don't take it, that's their choice.

So, with all of that in mind, let's say that you're the end-user and you're looking for a site full of information about the Paleo diet. You're considering going on it, and you want to find a bunch of recipes and enough information to get started. So, you run a Google search and you see a result for "Rock Solid Eating". You think it's a clever title and you decide to check the site out.

What would you want to see, and – more importantly – what would you not want to see?

People are looking for very specific things when they go to a website. First, they scan it to see if it looks legitimate. People are not dumb, and they know what scam websites look like. Blank websites or websites without character do not strike them as legitimate, no matter how DIY you're trying to come off. You need to do what you can in order to establish both a professional image and a professional design for yourself.

We'll go on with this analogy in a second, but for right now, I need to mark a really important set of distinctions here: voice. The voice that you speak to your user in makes a really big difference. You can't switch voices all the time either. You need to find a voice and stick to it.

Anyway, now imagine that you're the end user again. You found this site, it looks professional, and you decide to dip into some posts and see what this Paleo thing is about. You start reading a recipe: would you as the end user trust your site at this point? Is everything about the site attractive enough to make you actually feel like you would want to follow the recipes that it describes? Does it make you feel like you're wanted there?

Now, imagine you're reading the recipe itself, and they're mentioning a product (the affiliate product) that helped them to complete it or the affiliate service that sent them the produce they used to make the recipe. What kind of phrasing would make you interested in picking up their product?

People who try to market things online make big mistakes because, too often, they sound like marketers. They don't sound lax, nor do they sound like they know what they're talking about; they just sound like guinea pigs pressing keys a thousand times trying to make a commission selling a product they don't believe in.

If you want to sell things to humans, then, believe it or not, you have to act like a human – a real human being, not somebody who types "ACT NOW!!!!!! And you'll get a FIFTY percent discount – this DEAL WON'T LAST LONG!!" trying to sell a product. That's not good, and though my example just now is hyperbole, there genuinely are internet marketers out there who completely fail because they just don't know how to market their products. That's a shame, and you need to be smarter than to let that happen to you.

Now imagine that you're the user again, and you've read a couple of recipes and you like what you see. You've decided to give the Paleo diet a go, and you want to follow this site and know when they post new things. What can you do to make it as easy as possible for a user to keep up with you? Do you post your Facebook, YouTube, and other social media links very clearly on the header so that they can find it and get to those channels readily?

These are all factors that you need to consider when you're working on your site. If your site isn't really straightforward for the end users, then your site is not really worth anything at all. You have got to get into the head of the people who will be using your site so that you can make intelligent design choices.

With that, we've now reached the end of the book. The takeaway from this chapter needs to be that you carefully consider everything about your user's experience. It's really not complicated to be a good marketer, all that you have to do is think about how you would want to be taken into the site if you were just a common user.

Investing money is a requirement for an affiliate to make money. Buying traffic is a way for an affiliate to drive up the volume and to scale business. Traffic is driven to a website landing page, a website, link, or advertorial of a campaign for the affiliate is the goal. To generate and but this traffic, you may be wondering where to go. There are several different places you can go to that offer different types of potential customers. Your niche requires a specific audience, so it is important to choose a source that will provide you with the right people and context to look at your promotion.

AdWords: Keywords are words readers look for most often in search engines. This means that they have shown interest in a certain topic. This particular resource was one of the firsts to let affiliates reach about 70% of the search traffic globally. There are several tools offered which allows you to choose the right one for your campaign. There are some drawbacks, such as the strict rules regarding certain affiliate links and the expensive costs associated with certain keywords or subjects.

Bing: Bing.com is a search engine that offers Bing Ads for affiliates to advertise through. It does not generate as much traffic as AdWords, but it is not as strict and less expensive.

7Search: This advertising network allows you to promote a variety of vertical search engines including mobile capabilities. Other sites associated with 7search include bestsearch.com, finditquick.com, kijji.com, Kijiji.ca, and the freedistionary.com.

Social media: Social media is the advertising spot of choice right now. This platform allows you to contact and engage large amounts of people quickly. It also allows you to develop an interest in a product easily. This low-cost option capitalizes on the impulsive sharing of content from the users who pass on information they think is valuable to their community.

Facebook: Facebook Ads are one of the most popular resources for traffic. There is a large customer base, a variety of promotional options, and latitude for creativity and personalization. You can set goals anywhere from generating website clicks and image or video post sponsorships to generating leads, downloads of an app, or optimizing conversions. This resource allows you to identify your target audience regarding social media interests and behaviors and create a method for tracking and growing a base of audience members. To use this, you will need a free Facebook account and purchase traffic for little investment. Facebook does have rules regarding niches of a sexual nature and other topics, like cryptocurrency.

YouTube: This is the most used video-sharing platform currently. The collaboration with AdWords allows you to promote your video on YouTube by showing your promotion before or during a video or in the search results within YouTube. Influencers are the main users of this resource, but many businesses have seen success using this resource by increasing traffic and sales. It is a great resource for those that wish to increase profits using video marketing.

Twitter: Branding is what the Twitter platform is mainly used for currently. The streams of potential users that a brand targets can include images from Twitter advertising easily. There is a high cost associated with this ease and if you are looking mainly for conversion, it may not be the best platform for you. It is also a challenge because there is limited opportunity for writing information to a potential customer. It is a growing influence, so it is worth looking into and trying.

LinkedIn: If you are targeting B2B conversions, this is an advertising platform for you. It is an attractive resource because it is one of the few platforms that is aimed at almost solely professionals in various fields. LinkedIn ads offer the ability to pay for clicks and views with visibility on a variety of devices.

Prices can be considered high but because of its specificity, it can be a good generator.

Instagram: One of the newer social resources, this platform is already gaining traction as one of the most used traffic resources. You can generate clicks, promote app downloads, or interact with posts thanks to the integration with Facebook ads. This audience is typically young, and influencers are the ones that drive their purchase decisions. The ads are visible on mobile apps for Android and iOS devices.

Pinterest: A women-frequented site, this resource most successfully promotes clothing, furniture, and kitchen items. Sponsored pins are a method of promotion you can purchase. These are images with links attached to them that show up in the feeds or searches of targeted audiences or based on specific keywords.

Writing rules for success

These rules are here to shorten the learning curve and bring on your first sale earlier. Dedicating the months of preparation and dedication is important to the success of your blog. This requires more than just exciting concepts for articles. Commitment, preparation, and attention are all required consistently and cannot be neglected.

There is immense competition, with new content hitting the web every day. The good news is that not all of these will stay long or sell anything. Low traffic will kill off some of the competition within only a few months. Following set guidelines and utilizing good strategies to develop, monitor, and keep up your blog will improve your opportunity for success. By having an established blog that lasts a longer amount of time, you develop a reputation and potentially open the opportunity for consulting on blogging subjects. The following guidelines are here to help set you up for success. They are here to help you steer clear of common mistakes and risks almost every blogger face.

Make a great first impression: It matters. This means that the content is not enough. You need to have an attractive layout with good graphics to partner with the expert content. Choose a good theme that can showcase the site's content in a functional and an easy-to-navigate manner. Free templates from web hosting companies are nice to begin, it is important to decide if the template will allow you the ability to work with your demands. Decide if it is flexible enough to handle things like regular updates or has the ability to work with plugins and widgets. A function is critical to the theme and template. It needs to work with the latest version of WordPress.

Graphics are constantly improving for blogs. If you need to use a premade theme, consider opting for a premium one. These often have more functions and offer many demos. These demos are there to assist in developing strong graphics for the site.

Sometimes these are already created and can be added to your site easily.

Graphics partner is content: It is essential. This can be considered the heart of the blog; the thing that keeps it all going. Return traffic is a result of your content that is accurate, readable, and informative. A true mark of credibility is when a reader chooses to use your blog as a reference for information. Sometimes the authors get too caught up in the graphics and lack the attention to the content. Sometimes they get lazy and copy content. If a blog or website is caught plagiarizing content, they will receive a penalty. It is not worth it, no matter how exciting a topic is. Having useful and original content will grow your readership and improve your SEO. Search engines will list articles with over 1,500 words higher, especially when this detailed content is produced regularly on your site.

Organization leads to success: Making your blog easy to navigate for your readers is important. You can use a tool like WordPress to help you be more efficient in this manner. The different features in WordPress that you can use to make it easier for your readers to browse topics without difficulty include:

Widgets: Layout your sidebar for your reader. Offer links with labels such as suggested reading or most popular posts. If you are offering a FAQ-type post, consider having it listed here.

Tags and categories: Topics that interest your readers can be easy to access with good categories and tags in place.

Lend your expertise to others: Guest blogging is a valuable tool for increasing you and your blog's credibility. It also drives more readers to your site. Reaching out to other bloggers that cover your niche and requesting to guest blog for them on a one time or consistent basis is an easy way to make your own blog successful. This method does require you to write in the manner of the other bloggers and requires that you pay extra close attention to your professionalism and grammar. Choosing guest blogging as one of the promotional strategies is often a wise choice.

Reply and engage: When a reader takes the time to comment on your article or asks you a question, take the time to respond to them. This interaction is crucial. The more you interact and respond, the more people will comment and reach out. Your readers will feel that you listen to them and that you notice them. Simply recognizing their concerns can sometimes rectify conflicts or mistakes. This also fosters trust and an increase in referrals. Your readers will then start driving traffic to your site for you. The comment section on your blog is also a mini-community. Use this area to grow and foster a strong community, which is essential for brand development.

Be social: Immediate and effective interaction with your readers is now possible thanks to social media. It is a valuable tool for a successful blogger. Developing social media accounts on popular networks helps establish a strong audience for your site, creating a loyal readership that comes back again and again. These sites also help you promote your blog to potential new readers. The concept of going "viral" means that content on social media is bounced quickly between large groups of users on sites. This can be powerful for brand development.

Help others help you: Having social media buttons on the bottom of your articles lets your readers share your content for you. This means that they are reaching to their circle and beyond on your behalf, potentially driving new readers to your site. Many host sites and themes offer this function, which means you will not have to install anything additional to get this on your site. If you do select a theme without this function, follow the guidelines from your host site to learn how to add them. You do not want to miss out on this opportunity!

Link building is nothing to scoff at: Connecting your articles to various other blogs or resources helps build a valuable network of allies. Driving traffic to another site typically facilitates them driving it back to you in return. Do this sparingly, only linking to real sites with valuable information. Providing too many links or links that lead to irrelevant topics can be harmful to your content and credibility.

Up your ranking on Google with SEO knowledge: In order to get free traffic to your site, you need to get high on Google's list. WordPress offers plugins to help optimize SEO with tools like Yoast SEO. To be successful at affiliate marketing, it is essential that you learn and understand SEO.

Quick and easy are good terms: This means that your site does not take a long time to load. You can do this by selecting a hosting provider that values loading time as well. SiteGround is an example of a hosting provider that is excellent for support and performance. W3 Total Cache is an example of another tool that has been developed to help sites remain quick. Also, remember to choose tools on your site that can accommodate large increases in traffic. You do not want your site crashing, as it gets flooded with visits after a successful post!

Conclusion

Okay, we've come a long way and we've covered a lot, it's now time for you to get serious and start writing blog posts, and do all the other things that we discussed to get your blog in gear, like master your host's system, master WordPress, master Google Webmasters, and master your Autoresponder. And if you do all that, nothing can stop you! You will be an unstoppable freight train headed on track to becoming a blogging superstar.

We're talking raving fans, and nothing but first class airfare accommodations for you! And when you eat, of course, you can eat anything you want! Because you are a blogger!

The whole world caters to you, and you have options galore at your fingertips! Because you are a blogger!

And when you stop by your local favorite pizzeria, it's nothing but the best seat in the house for you, they keep it reserved for you, they keep it fresh! Fresh for you! Fresh for the blogger. Because you are a very special customer indeed! They treat you special! They treat you like the deserving fine blogger that you are! Because you are a blogger!

Yes, it's nothing but the very best for you!

However, you have a duty, and your duty is to your followers, they expect top-notch content, and they expect it in a timely fashion, so you'd better make sure that you always get out those blog posts on time! Failure to publish your blog posts on time is simply not an option!

It's funny how loyal followers so quickly turn into a rabid pack of hungry beasts if you miss a blog post!

But you get those blog posts all out on time and they're all perfect, just the way your fans like them. And your fans love you for it! Because you are a blogger!

Who wants to plug into a 9 to 5 anyway? That's not the lifestyle you want to live! You want to live life on your terms, your way. It's your way or no way! Because you are a blogger!

We're all looking forward to reading your blog posts, we're all looking forward to seeing what you've got!

It's time to make it happen!

See you in the blogosphere!

CPSIA information can be obtained
at www.ICGtesting.com
Printed in the USA
LVHW081045141120
671122LV00041B/367

9 781801 119337